FROM ROSH PINA AND DEGANIA
TO DIMONA
A HISTORY OF CONSTRUCTIVE ZIONISM

D1571916

Yosef Gorny

FROM ROSH PINA AND DEGANIA TO DIMONA

A HISTORY OF CONSTRUCTIVE

ZIONISM

MOD Books   Tel-Aviv

FROM ROSH PINA AND DEGANIA TO DIMONA
A HISTORY OF CONSTRUCTIVE ZIONISM
by
YOSEF GORNY

English translation by John Glucker

English Series Editor: Shmuel Himelstein

ISBN 965-05-0447-8

Computerized phototypesetting & printing: Naidat Press Ltd.
Printed in Israel

MOD Books — P.O.B. 7103, Tel-Aviv 61070, ISRAEL

Contents

INTRODUCTION

The purpose of this series of lectures, originally broadcast on Israel Army Radio, is to inform the members of the general public of the course of Zionist settlement in Eretz Israel (Palestine), to deepen their understanding of the enormous difficulties with which it had to contend, and to make the readers aware of the significance of constructive Zionism as an enterprise of the entire Jewish people, with all its different classes, cultures and Diasporas.

The stormy present has had an influence on what historians choose to study and has focused public attention on certain chapters in the history of our people and of Jewish settlement in Eretz Israel before the establishment of the State. Continuing political tension has prompted research into Zionism and international politics concerning Eretz Israel. Israel's wars with the Arab states have concentrated attention on the Arab-Israeli conflict form the beginning of the settlement movement. Inter-party struggles in the present have aroused interest in political controversies of the past. Present-day individualistic tendencies have strengthened curiosity in the lives and deeds of the early Zionist leaders. Inter-communal tensions have encouraged research into the culture and the contribution to Zionism of non-Ashkenazic communities. The increased strength of Zionist activism among certain religious groups has brought about an attempt at revision concerning the part played by religious groups, including the "Old Yishuv" (the long-established Jewish community in Eretz Israel before the beginning of Zionist settlement) in the Jewish national revival movement in Eretz Israel. Among all these studies, the position of the Zionist activity of the deepest national significance, that of the Jewish construction enterprise in Eretz Israel, has suffered. And why is that? It is hard to say. Perhaps it is because of the "dullness" of the subject as opposed to the others. Perhaps it is because the Israeli public in the 1980's, when Zionism celebrated its centenary, has lost interest in the building enterprise, which it now takes for granted. In any event, it is just because of this loss of interest that it must be stressed again and again that the Jewish people owes a very great debt to those "dull" people, those few who started their journey at Rosh Pina, travelled through Degania and reached Dimona. Through their acts, their suffering, their failures and their achievements, they express more than anything else the deepest significance of the Zionist revolution. It is this that I wished to discuss with the reader in this volume.

The Zionist revolution has a special place among the national cultural movements of the modern age. It encompassed within itself most of the experiences undergone by the nations and states of the modern period, but operated in incomparably worse conditions and with incomparably fewer resources than the others. Zionism was a national movement — but without a homeland, and a movement of migration from Europe — but without enormous areas for subsistence like those in the U.S.A., Canada, or Australia. It was a settlement enterprise — but one lacking the state assistance which the governments of Italy, Germany, or Japan gave to their citizens whom they wished to settle in the countries under their control. The Zionist movement wished to build a different, better, and more just society, as did other revolutionary movements, but, while they planned to change a society and an economy that already existed, Zionism was forced to build everything from the beginning. It seems that, more than any other social revolution, Zionism was bound up in the personal revolution of individual people, and that its character was established, to a greater degree than that of others, by the actions of small numbers.

Introduction

In the history of national settlement movements, constructive Zionism stands out for its *unique character*, and in the history of the Jewish people, it is conspicuous by its *success*. Among the various attempts to establish areas of Jewish settlement, such as in Argentina at the end of the nineteenth century; the Crimea in Russia in the 1920's; and Birobidjan in the Far East, on the border of the U.S.S.R. and China, at the beginning of the 1930's; only the Eretz Israel project was crowned with success. And it should be remembered that from the beginning the other projects enjoyed more generous support than did that obtained by the Zionist enterprise. Immediately after the publication of the Balfour Declaration, the Zionist leaders also hoped that Great Britain would give active and practical assistance in the building of the national home, but this hope was disappointed while still in its infancy.

Zionism was from the start a *voluntary* settlement and construction enterprise of the Jewish people alone. Moreover, in contrast to every other activity of the Jewish people, members of all communities and cultures took part in the Zionist construction enterprise. Thus the theory of Jewish *historical cooperation* became a fact, in a way unequalled since the dispersion of the nation in 70 C.E. This cooperation was not experienced by any Jewish group outside the State of Israel. And even though this cooperation was accompanied by tensions, frictions, feelings of frustration and a sense of alienation, all these divisive phenomena were anti-Zionist in character, and cannot negate the value and the historic achievement of Jewish Zionist construction in Eretz Israel.

I referred to the original series of broadcasts as "conversations," because I wanted not only to teach the general public something about the past, but also to discuss with it the unique quality of the historic experience which we are living through today. Therefore, while editing these words for print, I have tried to keep to their spoken, conversational style, with its description, analyses, and even hesitations. And if this modest little book helps to contribute to the readers' continued interest in the subject, I shall be most satisfied.

Yosef Gorny

I.

The Theoretical Foundations of Zionism

At this time the Zionist movement has been in existence for just over a century. After one hundred years of ideas, action, failures and successes, now that Zionism has apparently achieved its goal, it still gives rise to controversy and still stands at the center of the existence of the Jewish people and as a focus for its attention. This fact in itself seems to require an explanation.

It is worth noting that, of the great rivals of the Zionist movement and those movements which forcefully rejected it, some have disappeared from the scene of Jewish history, while others have come to terms with its existence or have decided to identify with it. We shall list them one after the other, beginning with the most extreme. Agudat Israel saw an alternative to Zionism in orthodox religious Jewish existence in the Diaspora until the coming of the Messiah. But Agudat Israel in the State of Israel, which is a Zionist state, has accepted Zionism in practice, if not in principle.

Another theory, that of "autonomism," the brainchild of the Jewish historian Simon Dubnow, believed in the possibility of national Jewish existence in the Diaspora within the framework of national cultural autonomy in the various Jewish centers, including Eretz Israel as but one of these. This theory disappeared even before the Holocaust, and was unrealistic even before that tragedy struck the Jewish people.

The rejecters on the left were the various kinds of non-Zionist

11

Jewish socialists, especially the Bund, which believed that within a future classless society the Jewish national problem would vanish, as would anti-Semitism. In such a situation, the Bund believed, the Jews could maintain a kind of cultural autonomy, to which they were entitled as a cultural group possessing certain national characteristics. This theory also failed tragically, and not only as a result of the Holocaust. It failed in the Soviet Union, where its supporters were scattered to the four winds. It also failed in the United States, where it was swallowed up in American society, a more open society which does not recognize national organization.

Those, too, who believed that the Jews needed a homeland, but did not believe that Eretz Israel was capable of becoming that homeland once more, those who sought territory for the Jews as a place in which they could build their lives normally (and among them there were also Zionists), also experienced failure even before the Second World War.

Even those who believed in integration, which would come about as a result of Jewish emancipation, suffered a tragic fall, mainly in Europe. A good example of this is the Jews of Germany between the two World Wars, who achieved the greatest degree of equality, involvement and integration of all the Jews of Europe. Their tragic fate illustrates the failure of the believers in emancipation.

Finally, we shall mention those who opposed Zionism, but came to terms with it and now identify with it. We refer here to the Reform Movement, which started out as an anti-nationalist, anti-Messianic religious movement and later also became anti-Zionist. But since the establishment of the State, and even during the struggle to establish it, the Reform Movement accepted the principles of Zionism and now belongs to the Zionist movement, just as other Jewish organizations in the western world belong to it. Today Reform's strong national position acts as one of the barriers against assimilation.

From all these points of view there is no doubt that Zionism is a relative success story. I say relative because it is engulfed by problems, is faced by crises, and is now in perhaps one of the most difficult times in its history. Zionism is nevertheless worthy of study and we shall study certain aspects of it, if not all its variations.

What was the Zionist movement originally? It had many different faces. It was a movement of national cultural revival, which arose to save the Jewish people from assimilation. It was a political organization, which struggled for national self-determination. It was a constructive enterprise, the aim of which was to build a normal society for the Jewish people. Out of these I have chosen as the subject of these chapters the constructive aspect of the Zionist movement, and we shall concentrate on the theory and action of building a society. We shall survey this building of a society throughout nearly one hundred years, from the First Aliyah (wave of Jewish immigration to Eretz Israel), from the days of the first settlements, to the mass aliyah that followed the establishment of the state, to the development towns. Therefore, I have called these chapters "From Rosh Pina and Degania to Dimona."

What is unique about the Zionist movement among the national movements of Europe, which developed there mainly in the nineteenth century? It certainly was one of a kind. It did not aim at liberating a homeland, as, for instance, the national movement in Poland, because it did not yet have a homeland. It did not aim at uniting a state, as the national liberation movement in Germany, because it did not have even part of a state. It was, first of all, a movement of return to the homeland. No other national movement in Europe had to face a problem such as this. For Zionism, unlike all the other national liberation movements of Europe, return to the homeland was a condition for liberation. Another condition for national liberation was the creation of a national economy.

Zionism was faced by a task that no other national movement had to face. It is true that the progressive national movements also spoke of social reforms, but for Zionism the problem was, first of all, that of building a different Jewish society: the transformation of Jewish society into a society of workers who were self-supporting and capable of living independently of any other nation. The building of the society became a condition for national existence, and the need to build the society and to return to the homeland also

13

influenced the political aspect. I shall only suggest here that the relationship with Great Britain, the ruling power in the region, was affected to a very great degree by Zionism's dependence on immigration and the need to buy land. If the nation had been living in its own country and if it had been in possession of the land, the relationship would also have been completely different. But this is just a brief aside, not connected with the subject of this volume.

The beginning of Zionism as a national movement was in "Hibbat Zion" (Love of Zion), which was the movement which arose in Eastern Europe — in Russia — at the time of the pogroms, and at other times. I differentiate between the time of the pogroms and other times because I wish to stress that this movement was not founded simply because of the pogroms. Firstly, nationalist ideas preceded the pogroms; secondly, the pogroms did not lead directly to Eretz Israel and to the national movement. The pogroms acted as a spur and as a goad, but the direction taken by different people was determined by other factors.

One should, therefore, distinguish between factors that pushed, like Jewish distress, and those that pulled, like the *link with Eretz Israel*, which was common to different groups: the Maskilim (emancipated, educated Jews), the young, and the nationalist Jewish middle class. This link was handed down to them from the sources, by history. They were also affected by intellectual trends in the non-Jewish world, that is by the nationalist movements.

What were the principles of Hibbat Zion? Its first principle was gradual return to the homeland. Hibbat Zion believed that Zionism signified a very long drawn-out process, the end of which could not be foreseen, and that the main thing was the existence and the working out of this process, which the Hovevei Zion (members of Hibbat Zion) saw as a great national act. But this process, the continuing national effort, was not directed toward settling any territory regardless of location, but toward the nation's historic fatherland, apart from which their Zionism had no meaning at all.

The second principle was the national unity of the Jewish people, and not only on a religious basis. One must understand that Hibbat Zion arose at a time when the process of secularization was penetrating ever deeper into the Jewish people, with ever-increasing strength. The big question then was in what way the unity of the Jewish people ought to be expressed. If the Jewish people had no territory, no common language, no political framework, and if even its religious foundation was becoming more shaky, what would express its unity? Hibbat Zion arose and gave an answer in its vision of national revival and a national movement directed toward the historic homeland. This trend towards national revival also included the revival of the Hebrew language and Hebrew culture.

The third principle was that of Hebrew labor, at which I hinted above. It was Hibbat Zion that raised the idea of productivization, of labor, principally of working the land — but not only working the land - as a condition of national revival and also as a way of redeeming the individual. The two things were bound up together. Hibbat Zion derived this principle from the Jewish "Haskalah" (Enlightenment) movement which preceded it, but with one great difference. Hibbat Zion "nationalized" the idea of independent labor, of Jewish labor, and turned it into the idea of Hebrew labor in Eretz Israel.

Another principle of Hibbat Zion can be called the "activist principle." Hibbat Zion put forward the idea of action in the national sphere, not only in terms of maintaining Jewish national existence in one way or another, but action directed toward the maintenance of national existence within the historic homeland. From this point of view, Hibbat Zion changed the Jewish tradition of expectation and passivity, which, even if we were to regard it as activism in the more traditional and religious terms, was becoming, in a world growing more and more secular, a passivity. It was Hibbat Zion that raised the idea of a national activism that was expressed, in its view, in immigration to Eretz Israel and in laying down the foundations of a productive society, mainly in the first settlements.

There were many different innovations in the appearance of Hibbat Zion. The first of these was that it adopted a defined national goal for itself. This goal was settlement of Eretz Israel, without determining the pace of this settlement or its dimensions. Hibbat Zion gave the national movement its target, to which everyone directed himself and to which all eyes turned, whether in criticism or in agreement.

The second innovation of Hibbat Zion was the clarification of the essential connection, the connection that could not be broken, between Jewish nationalism and its historic homeland. Throughout the entire period, even after Hibbat Zion had disappeared and merged into the Zionist movement, it and its leaders were never prepared to renounce the link between Eretz Israel and the Jewish people as an essential connection. They would not renounce this link even when troubles afflicted the Jewish people and territorial alternatives such as the Uganda plan appeared, and even when faced with Jewish suffering in the pogroms. Eventually this link, originally considered irrational, was proved to be the most realistic in history. The Jews were not prepared to invest in any other place the effort which they invested in Eretz Israel.

The third innovation brought about by Hibbat Zion, following on from the second, was that, by its adherence to Eretz Israel, it turned that country into the focus of the national debate within the Jewish people.

If we wish to evaluate the contribution of Hibbat Zion from the historical point of view, it would be hard to speak only of its achievements and unfair to speak only of its failures. I would define it thus: Hibbat Zion, which was founded as a movement of East European Jews and existed between the years 1882 and 1897 (until the foundation of the Zionist Federation under the leadership of Theodore Herzl), was a *movement* that failed, but an *idea* that succeeded.

It failed in many different areas. It failed because it did not succeed in arousing a widespread settlement movement; it failed to recruit people, or to recruit money. Its tragedy was that it was incapable of assisting the first settlers in any significant way. The one who saved the settlements was not Hibbat Zion, but a great Jewish benefactor with a very wide-reaching national outlook, Baron Edmond de Rothschild.

Hibbat Zion failed also because it did not nurture within its ranks a charismatic leadership with the strength and ability to draw the masses behind it, in particular to inspire the young. Neither did it succeed from the point of view of organization. Even when it did attempt to organize on a nationwide basis, the organization, founded formally in 1884, had no great practical, tangible significance. Nor did it succeed in founding a national organization that could expand beyond the geographical and cultural bounds of Eastern Europe, because the attempts to recruit the Jews of Western Europe to the ranks of Hibbat Zion almost all resulted in failure. Hibbat Zion failed in what Herzl promised just a year later. But Hibbat Zion succeeded as an idea in those senses which I indicated above, in putting forward certain principles of national thought and action, which did not vanish together with the disappearance of Hibbat Zion as an organized movement.

Moreover, the success of a social movement in history is measured not only by its achievements in its own time, but also by its attraction of followers to continue in its path, and by its ability to pass on the principles of its world view to the generations that follow it. It seems to me that from this point of view Hibbat Zion succeeded, for its followers arose, in strange and unintentional ways, in the form of the "halutzim" (Jewish pioneers in Eretz Israel), who came in the waves of immigration that followed. Despite the fact that they, so to speak rebelled against its ideology, particularly Ahad Ha'am's version of it, in practice they followed in its path.

It must be stressed that from the time when Hibbat Zion was founded in 1882 until 1924, when the immigration regulations of the U.S.A. were tightened and the number of those entering was drastically restricted, Jewish migrants of the time had a free choice. Only a very small part of the great flood of Jewish migrants came to Eretz Israel. But those who did come at that time fulfilled in different ways the basic ideas of Hibbat Zion, namely the return to Eretz Israel in order to build in it, through labor, a national Jewish society. And so in this period, when the Jews had this free choice, the *few* laid down the foundations of the state for the *many*.

I intend to show how the constructive enterprise, which began in the First Aliyah and continued in the Second, Third and Fourth

Aliyahs and those that come later, not only built in Eretz Israel a Jewish society different from that in the Diaspora, but also laid the foundations of the political society, that is the State of Israel.

II.

Eretz Israel Before
The First Aliyah

In the first chapter we considered the principal ideas of Zionism as a national movement in nineteenth century Europe. This present chapter is concerned with the social and economic situation in Eretz Israel before the First Aliyah, both the Jewish and the non-Jewish situation.

From the beginning of the sixteenth century Eretz Israel had been part of the Ottoman Empire. The three hundred years since 1516, when Eretz Israel was conquered by the Turks, until the middle of the nineteenth century, had been a period of inactivity and general backwardness in all spheres: economic, social, cultural and administrative. But in the middle of the nineteenth century there began a process of change, which we call modernization, when the influence of the western world penetrated the region.

On the eve of the First Aliyah, then, the situation in Eretz Israel was stable, but there were recognizable signs of change, leading to western progress. The land in the middle or late nineteenth century was, of course, not empty. The population in the mid-nineteenth century numbered about 400,000 inhabitants, mostly Sunni Moslems. The country had a traditional Moslem society, which was mainly agricultural. Between 70% to 80% of the inhabitants lived in villages and supported themselves from agriculture. About 20% to 30% lived in the various towns.

This agricultural society produced mainly for itself. Very little was produced for the market. It was a society which could be called, in a way, feudal. Under a law passed by the government in 1858, the farmers were obliged to register their holdings in land registers. Many of the peasants refrained from registering their plots with the authorities for fear of taxes. They therefore surrendered the right to register these holdings to the great families, who registered them in their own names. As a result, huge estates were created belonging to various families, some of which did not even live in the country. This is important to our discussion, because the later land purchases by the Jews were made, not from isolated peasants, but from these (sometimes absentee) estate-owners.

Agricultural production was limited mainly to subsidence and to some extent to supplying the towns. At this time there were two different types of towns; there were those like Jenin, Hebron, or Gaza, which were closely linked with an agricultural region and served as markets for agricultural produce. In contrast, Jaffa and, in particular, Jerusalem, had more of a commercial character, even including a certain international dimension.

Yet even in this markedly conservative society, both economically and culturally, the first signs of change appeared in the mid-nineteenth century. At the end of the eighteenth century, in 1799, Eretz Israel was brought into the sphere of western influence, as a result of Napoleon's invasion of the country. From then on the involvement to the European powers in Eretz Israel had continually increased. This involvement reached its peak in 1831, with the invasion of Eretz Israel by Mehmed Ali, the ruler of Egypt, and the intervention of the British, who forced him to withdraw.

Another way in which the powers intervened was through the capitulations arrangement. This had already begun in the sixteenth century and its effect was to exclude citizens of European states from the jurisdiction of Ottoman law and to place them under the protection of foreign consuls. Under this arrangement, the powers of which continually increased during the nineteenth century as Turkey became weaker, foreign citizens were in effect excluded from the sphere of Ottoman imperial sovereignty.

These were the political changes. As far as social changes were concerned, these began taking place at a far faster rate than in the past. The central government was increasingly strengthened, this centralization being one of the identifying features of a modern state. There was some improvement in road communications, another of the features of a modern state. New economic sectors were developed, such as the citrus industry. A sort of "international economy" was created in Jerusalem, nourished mainly by the crowds of pilgrims who came to Eretz Israel every year, mainly from Eastern Europe, and around this phenomenon of pilgrimage there grew up a tourist economy. The Templars founded their first settlements. They were religious German immigrants, who built agricultural settlements in Eretz Israel and developed modern agriculture in them. All these were signs of modernization among the non-Jewish community in Eretz Israel.

What was the situation among the Jews? The new immigrants, who began to arrive from 1882 onwards, referred to the Jewish population of Eretz Israel which had lived there for hundreds of years as the "Old Yishuv." On a simple level, the term "Old Yishuv" was meant to indicate those who had been in the country before the new wave of immigration, whose members formed the "New Yishuv." But it is also capable of another interpretation, where "Old Yishuv" referred to those who were adherents of old values and what was considered the antiquated way of the past, the "Guardians of the Walls," so to speak — the walls of tradition. The term can also be interpreted as a critical evaluation by those who saw themselves as innovators and introducers of a new spirit and new ways into Eretz Israel, as opposed to those frozen in their conservatism.

Among the Jewish community there were two noticeable trends. On the one hand, there was respect for tradition and rigid conservatism. On the other hand, there were changes and tendencies leading to a different development. In the middle of the nineteenth century, more precisely in 1856, the Jewish community in Eretz Israel numbered 10,500 people. Of these 5,700 lived in Jerusalem, where they made up about one third of the entire population of the city. In Safed there lived 2,100, in Tiberias 1,500, in Hebron 400, and in Jaffa 400. About a generation—twenty-five years — later, in 1881, right on the threshold of the First Aliyah, the

Jewish community numbered 25,000 souls, 15,000 of them in Jerusalem. The proportion of Jews in the general urban population stood at 45%. Moreover, by 1881 the Jews were by far the largest urban community.

There was a communal division within the Old Yishuv between the Sephardim — who originally came from Spain or from Asian countries — and the Ashkenazim (Jews from Germany and Eastern Europe). Until the middle of the nineteenth century the majority was Sephardi, but from the middle of the century an Ashkenazi majority began to appear. On the eve of the First Aliyah, in 1881, the Ashkenazim comprised 60% of the Jewish community in Eretz Israel.

The social division within this community was not only into two groups, the Ashkenazim and Sephardim, but there were also internal divisions within these groups themselves. A distinction existed between the Sephardim and the Mograbim, those who came from North Africa, and there was a clear and pronounced difference among the Ashkenazim between the Hasidim (members of the Hasidic movement) and the Perushim (Mitnagdim).

Relations between the two communities, the Sephardim and the Ashkenazim, were usually tense. There was a linguistic difference between those who spoke Spanish or Arabic and those who spoke only, or mainly, Yiddish. There was a clear difference in culture and there was a power struggle for control over the communities. Apart from particular cases of contact between individuals, and here and there even marriages, generally the differences and the tensions between the two groups remained.

There was also a cultural difference between the communities, that was expressed in their attitude to financial aid from abroad. The Old Yishuv was maintained to a large extent by the "Halukah" — the contributions exacted from the Jews by envoys from Eretz Israel to allow those living in Eretz Israel to study Torah (the Bible and Oral Law), on behalf of all the People of Israel. While the Halukah was not the only source of finances in the community, it could not support itself without it, and this was the important distinction. There was a great difference between the methods by which the Sephardim and the Ashkenazim distributed the Halukah funds. The Sephardim divided the money: one third went to those in need, one third to scholars, and one third to public institutions. Among the Ashkenazim it was divided equally to every individual. This public was usually poor, or even very poor. In contrast to this individual poverty, the relative prosperity of the public sector was all the more conspicuous. Public institutions, like synagogues and yeshivas (religious seminaries) were sometimes magnificent buildings. This too illustrates the priorities in the use of the Halukah funds, which put public institutions before individual welfare.

As stated earlier, signs of change could also be noted within the Old Yishuv. Involvement by philanthropic institutions in the Old Yishuv began in the middle of the nineteenth century. These bodies set up various institutions, which, by their nature, led to modernizing changes. In 1854 the Rothschild family founded a hospital. In 1860 the Alliance Israelite Universelle began operating within the Old Yishuv. In 1870 the Alliance founded Mikveh Israel, which was intended as an agricultural school to train the Jews for work on the land. The general purpose of the Alliance was to help the Jewish community to become productive, in order to assist its integration into society as a whole. Mikveh Israel should be seen not as the start of Zionist agricultural activity, but as a vocational school, intended to train Oriental Jews — those from Asia and North Africa — as well as those from Eastern Europe, in agricultural work.

With the founding of this school, an element of modernization had, of course, penetrated the Old Yishuv. This was also the case with regard to the new neighborhoods built in the Old Yishuv, particularly in Jerusalem. Some were built as the result of philanthropic initiatives, some at the initiative of public organizations abroad, and some at the initiative of wealthy families who were part of the Old Yishuv. These neighborhoods became Mishkenot Sha'ananim, founded by Montefiore; Mahaneh Israel, founded by the western Mograbi North African community; Nahalat Shivah, founded by the Rivlin and Solomon families; and,

23

finally, the biggest neighborhood of all, Me'ah She'arim, founded in 1874. There was also a trend toward productivization in the Old Yishuv, which was seen in a transition toward productive labor. During the generation 1856-1881, the proportion of income-earners who supported themselves by their labors —principally by crafts — grew from 4% to 15% of the community as a whole.

There were also early signs of agricultural labor, such as the Montefiore citrus groves. There was even an attempt by the Jews of Safed to found an agricultural settlement. The crowning achievement of the modernizing, productivist trend in the period was the laying of the foundations of the first agricultural settlement in Eretz Israel. Petah Tikva was founded in 1878, before the First Aliyah, by three men from the Old City of Jerusalem: Joel Moshe Solomon, Joshua Stampfer, and David Gutman, who came from Hungary and settled in Jerusalem. It is true that this attempt did not succeed, and it required new immigrants, who came with the wave of "Hovevei Zion" (members of Hibbat Zion), to revive the settlement, but it was nevertheless the crowning achievement of the process of productivization and modernization within the Old Yishuv.

In view of these developments, the question is raised as to what extent these changes were forerunners of the national movement. That is a difficult question. In all these changes one can discern the first signs of what later became the activities of the national movement. Nevertheless, however much those changes may have been important on their own account, it is doubtful whether they were forerunners of the national movement, since they all originated in the desire to improve conditions for the Jews living in the Old Yishuv, particularly in Jerusalem. These changes were intended to improve their situation in a number of different fields: in housing, in their economic position, in education, and in broadening the range of occupations open to them. It was in order to increase their income that they also went out to the countryside — to the settlements.

But all of these indications and all these efforts, both of the Jews of the Old Yishuv and of the philanthropists, had no clear national

24

policy bent on changing the face of the Yishuv and on constituting a sort of pioneer for the Jewish people, which would migrate in its masses to Eretz Israel. There was no such policy, and so a unique awakening was required, one that in fact came from abroad, to put this clear policy into action.

Sometimes there are different purposes behind the same activities. These purposes can be tested, not only by their own times, but also by their future. In my opinion, the Old Yishuv was not capable of becoming a basis for a national movement. And so the national movement which sprang up in Eastern Europe pushed it aside, becoming increasingly more powerful throughout the generations. Whatever it accomplished, it did as a result of policy, and so it achieved the aim it had set itself.

To demonstrate this, I shall take as examples the Halukah on the one hand, and the aid which the later settlers received on the other. People often tend, either from lack of understanding or from a desire to be provocative, to compare the Halukah of the Old Yishuv with the assistance which the settlers received from Baron de Rothschild, and the aid of the national funds for the settlement movement as a whole. I shall devote some lines to this matter in future chapters, but I wish to stress here that there was a qualitative difference in the intentions behind the two types of aid. The Halukah was intended to maintain and preserve a community and not to alter anything in it. Its purpose was to help to support the Jews who lived in Jerusalem, whose aim it was to pray for the people of Israel. On the other hand, the purpose of the aid given to the new settlement movement was to broaden the scope of settlement activity, so that it could be a basis for the absorption of the Jewish masses.

From this point of view, there is a qualitative difference between aid given to a society to preserve a historic situation, and aid given to a society that intends to change a historic situation. Even if in both cases the financial aid was not always used to the best advantage; even if in both cases this aid was accompanied by dubious behavior, such as the feathering of the nests of those closest to the purse strings; still the differences between them were like that between the old and the new. The old sanctified the past: it was an expression of Jewish continuity from the Diaspora; it intended to remain old; its very strength lay in being old. The new intended to change the Jewish situation that prevailed in the Diaspora. Its strength lay in its dynamism, in its desire for change. At this stage a great gulf stretched between the old and the new.

III.

The Period of The First Aliyah

In the previous chapter I alluded to the qualitative difference between the old and the new. In this chapter I shall turn to the new, to the wave of immigration of the First Aliyah, and shall attempt to understand both what it was and what it did.

The year 1882 was the turning point. In this remarkable year, the first Hebrew settlements in Eretz Israel were founded. It was these settlements that laid the foundations for the new Jewish society that grew up there, and so also for the State of Israel. And indeed Rishon le-Zion (the First in Zion), Petah Tikva (the Gate of Hope) and Rosh Pina (the Cornerstone) were what their names implied. They were the harbingers of revival; they proclaimed a new direction.

This took place in the period between 1882 and 1904. In the space of a generation, two waves of immigration reached their peak. The first came in 1882, following the pogroms in Russia. The second arrived in 1890-91, following new decrees, especially the expulsion of Jews from Moscow. The second wave was known as "Tyomkin's Aliyah" and to a certain degree it was different in its aims from the first wave. On this we will dwell more below.

It was far from the best time for immigration. The Turkish government was in the grip of suspicion regarding the intentions of the western powers. The Congress of Berlin in 1878 and the British conquest of Egypt in 1882 had aroused fears in the Turkish government that there were plans to dismantle the Ottoman

Empire, and so it regarded every western immigrant with suspicion. The Jews, therefore, became the objects of the government's suspicions.

Severe restrictions were imposed on immigration, but the Jews managed to get round them in various ways. One way was bribery, which was used on officials. The immigrants came mainly from Rumania and Russia. Their number was somewhere between twenty and thirty thousand. At exactly the same time, about a million and a half Jews migrated to the U.S.A. The flow of immigrants of Eretz Israel was only a thin trickle, compared with the mighty flood of Jewish migration to the United States. Precisely because of the limited numbers of immigrants, aliyah to Eretz Israel was not a matter of chance nor of compulsion, since the Jews could choose between aliyah to Eretz Israel and migration to the United States, the gates of which were at that time wide open to the Jews. The vast majority of the immigrants to Eretz Israel were married and with children, in their late thirties or forties, traditional, religious people. They could hardly be considered Maskilim; their education was traditional. These immigrants cannot be described as wealthy. Nearly all of them possessed moderate means or less. Among the immigrants of this aliyah, one group of young people stood out, a group known as Bilu: "O House of Jacob, let us arise and go" (Isaiah 2:5 — the name Bilu is an acronym of the Hebrew for this phrase). They were a group of idealistic students with a comprehensive nationalist outlook, who saw themselves as pioneers for the Jewish people and who planned to create a settlement. But they were very few, a few dozen, and they were not typical of the First Aliyah. The First Aliyah was the aliyah of the traditional Jewish *petit bourgeoisie*, and this was its largest and most important achievement.

How did this aliyah operate? First of all, it must be stressed that the initiative for aliyah did not come from any center, nor did the organization, the fund-raising, and the purchase of land. The movement still had no leader to inspire it; nor an organization to train the immigrants, to buy the land, and to make the immigration arrangements. The aliyah was mainly the result of spontaneous

28

local organization. There arose local associations that organized themselves and sent their people to settle in Eretz Israel. It is true that there was individual leadership. But it was limited, local, personal leadership. There was David Schub, a ritual slaughterer from Rumania, who fell in love with Eretz Israel, organized a group, bought land in Rosh Pina and migrated there at the head of his group. There was Zalman David Levontin, an accountant from Krementchug in the Ukraine, who organized a group of people, went on ahead of them as a pioneer, searched for acreage, and bought the lands of Rishon le-Zion.

Another characteristic of these people's activities was a lack of agricultural knowledge and a great deal of naivete. The first settlers in Petah Tikva in 1878 settled on the banks of the River Yarkon, because they thought that the river bank would be the best place for a settlement. They felt that since there were fish in the river, fishing would provide a useful addition to the family income. But the Yarkon had more mosquitoes than fish, and there was more malaria than income. This was one of the reasons for the failure of this settlement.

Rosh Pina, an area of beautiful mountainous scenery and pure air, was very far from the center. The people who went there did not realize that they were being sent off to the farthest corner of the country. Zichron Ya'acov, originally Zimmarin, was a lovely hill, looking out over the sea on one side and the mountains on the other. Those who bought it were impressed by the view, but did not realize that its ground was rocky and would require enormous labor to clear it of stones. Yesud Hama'aleh also lay on the banks of a lake, but mosquitoes hummed over its waters and malaria struck the residents. In the history of settlement in Eretz Israel, there is no example of suffering to equal that of the founders of Yesud Hama'aleh, or of the heroism of these simple people. They refused to abandon the place, although Baron de Rothschild, or, more precisely, his officials, put forward tempting offers of a transfer to another site. It was the same at Hadera, the settlement founded in the second wave of aliyah, also established on the edge of a marsh. It suffered from malaria as well, and was salvaged by the intervention of the baron, who paid with his money for draining the marsh. But the people, despite their sufferings, refused to leave.

The settlers endured very great trials in the early stages. Failure followed on failure. One of the most outstanding failures was the inability of these groups to organize communal labor among their members. The idea that the settlers should form a sort of cooperative, a work group based on principles of temporary, non-socialist, purely practical cooperation, failed. The idea failed because the composition of the settlement group was not homogenous as regards economic status. There were property owners and poor men and they could not cooperate and work together. The failure of the idea of communal labor was to a considerable degree the cause of the economic difficulties which beset the immigrants shortly after they settled on the land.

An additional difficulty was the limited amount of independent capital possessed by the settlers. They had no tools to assess how much they would have to invest in preparing the soil, and very quickly came to the brink of bankruptcy. Their appeals to their associations abroad were answered at first by a little aid, but later these associations were incapable of sending more money. The settlers were forced, therefore, to appeal to their guardian, to the one who could save them from total failure.

Before we turn to describing Baron de Rothschild's enterprise, which was a rescue operation for this settlement phase, let us first discuss the theoretical dimension of the First Aliyah. Not all the immigrants had all-embracing nationalist opinions, but a large number of them, perhaps the majority — both those who settled in agricultural villages and those who settled in towns — held traditional views, with certain new nationalist tendencies, principally to renew Jewish settlement in Eretz Israel.

But among them were also those who saw in this enterprise the beginnings of national revival. The names of the settlements: Rishon le-Zion, Petah Tikva, Rosh Pina, were not accidental. Levontin saw in his scheme at Rishon le-Zion a pioneering project, a precursor of Jewish settlement. The Biluim had an overall national vision. They believed that a Jewish Eretz Israel would arise only as a result of communal national effort; not only agricultural, but also industrial and even military. It is true that not all the first settlers in Eretz Israel had a definite, all-inclusive national vision, but the dynamic individuals and the dynamic groups among them, such as Bilu, did have an all-inclusive national conception and clear aims and purposes.

To what extent was it possible to achieve these aims? That was a different matter, and to clarify it we will describe the involvement of Baron de Rothschild, which was an example of the gap between the vision and the reality. This gap can be very tragic, for sometimes the broader the vision, the more comprehensive, the more sublime; the more tragic is the meeting with reality, for reality is resistant and holds unexpected surprises. The sandy soil of Rishon le-Zion, the rocks of Zimmarin, which later became Zichron Ya'acov, the malaria of Yesud Hama'aleh — these were the first surprises of the reality of Eretz Israel, and hurt the vision badly. The appeal to Baron Rothschild came, therefore, from the settlers themselves, or, more precisely, from the representatives of the settlers and of Hovevei Zion.

Undoubtedly, the baron's response to the settlers' cry for help was of a quite extraordinary historic significance. Now, who was Baron Rothschild? He was not a philanthropist of the usual type; he can be defined as a philanthropist with a national vision. He did not come to the aid of the settlers simply to support a few hundred Jewish families, who, whether or not by chance, happened to be in Eretz Israel. He did not come to their aid simply because these people had tried to become productive. He saw in this attempt, this experiment of a few settlements, the beginning of a possible way to a solution of the problem of the Jewish masses of Eastern Europe. He saw in these settlements models for future mass settlement. And so he invested a great deal of his money, time and interest in them.

The baron had a hard, paternalistic personality. He insisted on being heard and obeyed. He had his own ideas and was not prepared to suffer the independent opinions or opposition of the settlers. But his intentions were not only to do the best for them, but also to take steps that would have national significance.

The problem caused by the baron's involvement was that of the relations between the baron's officials (as his administrators were called) and the farmers. Unlike the baron, these officials had no national vision. They were nearly all French Jews, and even those of them born in Eastern Europe had been educated in France, and were men of assimilationist views who had assimilated themselves. They tended to be arrogant and viewed the Eastern European Jews with not a little contempt, seeing them as apprentices who needed to be led along the right path rather than as pioneers blazing a new trail for their people.

There are two possible ways to evaluate the work of the baron's officials, and they are both valid. From the economic point of view, their work was extremely valuable. With the aid of the baron's funds, they brought about an economic turning point in the settlements, when they put them on a basis of orchard cultivation. They improved working methods, introduced modern administrative techniques and gave the farmers an economic basis for their future support. It is true, however, that under their administration and their control of the settlements, the farmers were not independent. The baron's administration turned them, in effect, into his hired laborers, because they were paid, not according to their production, but according to prices and quotas fixed by the officials.

The evaluation of the social dimension is different. From this point of view, the emergence of the baron's officials was not positive, but negative. These officials created new standards for the settlements. They turned a society of courageous and independent people into one of dependents. In every regime of dependency there is a certain degree of social corruption, since it always creates those who are more or less intimate with it, those who enjoy the favors of the administration or the guardians, and those who are persecuted by them. Those who rebelled were severely punished, and with the baron's approval. Those who adjusted did well.

The officials also introduced another culture. They created a group with cultural and social attitudes different from the nationalist spirit that prevailed in the villages. French, the language they spoke, became a status symbol among many of the young people of the villages. Piano playing, later to be anathema to the members of the Second Aliyah, was a symbol of a certain mentality. Regarding Paris as the source of culture and desiring to travel there for higher education at the baron's expense, created an atmosphere different from the settlers' original nationalist spirit.

When we evaluate the baron's enterprise, therefore, we must consider both aspects of it, both the economic contribution and its success, and the social damage done, mainly by his officials, but also by the baron himself, since without him these things would not have happened.

It should be understood that the baron invested a great deal of money in this enterprise. If we compare his investment with that of the Hovevei Zion, the proportion is that of twenty to one. The baron invested 1,600,000 pounds sterling in the project, which was a colossal sum at that time. At exactly the same time, Hovevei Zion, on the other hand, invested only 80,000 pounds.

The baron's direct administration came to an end in 1900, when, for various reasons with which we shall deal later, he decided to transfer his assets to the Jewish Colonial Association (ICA), which was known in Eretz Israel as the Palestine Jewish Colonial Association (PICA). With the appearance of ICA in the villages, there began a new era in the history of the settlement movement, the period of the Second Aliyah.

IV.

The Social and Economic Balance of The First Aliyah

There were great differences between the administration of Baron Rothschild and the economic methods of administration used by PICA, both in approach and in conception. The baron transferred his assets to PICA at the height of an economic crisis, the vineyard crisis, and at the height of the rift with the farmers. He did not respond to their demands that he should hand over the properties for them to manage independently. The administrators of PICA had no national vision, as had the baron. They regarded the enterprise in a far more restricted light. For them, the settlers were a group of Jews occupied in productive labor. The PICA managers believed that everything possible should be done to improve the settlers' conditions and to enable them to support themselves from their labor, so that as soon as possible they would no longer need support from philanthropic or public funds.

For this reason they carried out some very harsh economic measures. They abolished the system of advance payments, fixed with no reference to the produce or to market prices, and introduced a system that took the market situation into account. They also gave the farmers loans on a commercial basis. The farmers had to repay these loans to the company with interest, not as in the days of the baron, when they were given grants. On the other hand, the directors of PICA did transfer more and more enterprises to the farmers' independent management, as, for example, the wineries, which eventually became farmers' cooperative enterprises.

PICA also became involved in settlement, but not for Zionist reasons. It was forced to deal with the problem of unemployed Jewish workers in the villages, who had no land and no means to buy farms. In this way PICA embarked on the settlement project in the Lower Galilee. But it insisted from the start that the farmers or settlers must adjust their way of life, their standard of living, and their working methods to those of the Arab peasants. In this way Yavniel, Sejera and Kfar Tabor were founded as farming settlements, based mainly on field crops. The standard of living in these villages was, of course, much lower than in the villages of Judea and Samaria, which were based on fruit plantations.

The PICA agronomists introduced new fruit crops. They varied the fruit growing economy and, as a result of this project, the citrus sector, which eventually became the main branch of the orchard economy, began to develop. It can be said that, in a paradoxical way, that non-Zionist, or even anti-Zionist, company, in its economic severity, in fact, did the settlements a great deal of good and thus even helped the Zionist enterprise.

In summing up the settlement activity that began with the First Aliyah, one comes to a number of interesting conclusions. In 1903, at the end of the First Aliyah period, there were about 6,000 Jews in the farming villages, about one fifth to one quarter of all the immigrants of that time. Thus it appears that the majority of the immigrants in that period did not come to settle on the land, but established themselves in the towns, just as they had done for generation after generation, both in Eretz Israel and elsewhere.

Altogether, twenty three farming villages were founded in that period, from Rosh Pina in the north to Gedera in the south. In these villages there were about 700 separate farms. The total area of land bought by Jews at that time amounted to 400,000 dunams (a Turkish land measurement, approx. 1,000 sq. m.) of which nearly 100,000 were in Transjordan. The land there was acquired by the baron and serves as evidence for his settlement vision. He viewed even these regions, including parts of the Golan, as possible settlement areas for the Jewish masses that would come later.

It is true that this area comprised only 1.5% of the total area of

Eretz Israel, but if we compare it with the total of land purchases made by the Zionist movement, it is certainly not small. In thirty years of activity in Eretz Israel, between 1908 and 1938, when restrictions were imposed on land purchase, the Jewish National Fund bought an area no larger than this, or possibly even smaller. When compared to the opportunities for buying land at that time and later, the land purchase of the First Aliyah by the baron and by private individuals was therefore a large-scale enterprise.

The economy of the villages on the coastal plain was based primarily on fruitgrowing, first and foremost of grapes, and after that, of olives, almonds and citrus fruits. In the Galilee, as mentioned, the villages lived on field crops. Geographically, the villages can be divided into four separate settlement blocks. The first were the villages of Judea, the biggest of which were Petah Tikva, Rishon le-Zion, and Rehovot. Rehovot, founded in the second immigration wave of 1890-91, was to some extent unusual. It was founded by Maskilim, pupils of Ahad Ha'am, of the "Sons of Moses" association. It was planned from the start to be based on Hebrew labor and to revive the Hebrew language, and it had a fair degree of success. The second group were the villages of Samaria. The biggest of them were Zichron Ya'acov and the long-suffering Hadera, saved by the baron's intervention. The third block were the Lower Galilee villages of Sejera, Yavniel and Kfar Tabor. The last group comprised the settlements of the Upper Galilee: Rosh Pina, Yesud Hama'aleh and, later, Metula.

In this way, something like four blocks of settlement were created in Eretz Israel. But it should be emphasized that the creation of these blocks was not premeditated. Developments took place in accordance with the possibilities of land purchase. During the second wave of the First Aliyah, in the days of Tyomkin and Hankin, when it looked as if immigration was reviving and thousands of Jews would come, an attempt was made to buy large, coordinated tracts of land. The possibility was raised of buying the Valley of Jezreel as a territorial and geographical link connecting the settlements of the Galilee with those of the coastal plain, and this was already a sign of a settlement strategy. But this enterprise —

this dream — did not succeed because of the political conditions of the time, and was revived only at the beginning of the 1920's, in the Third Aliyah.

The settlements can be divided according to size into three groups. The large ones numbered between 500 and 800 inhabitants. These were Petah Tikva, Rishon le-Zion, Rehovot, etc. The middle sized ones had between 150 and 400 inhabitants. They included Rosh Pina and Hadera. The small ones, between 15 and 150 people, were mainly the settlements founded by PICA.

It must be understood that not all the settlements were under the baron's supervision, and that, obviously, not all of them had been rescued by his efforts. Villages like Rehovot and Gedera were independent; Rehovot, because its settlers had independent capital, Gedera, because it enjoyed the exclusive support of the Hovevei Zion in Russia.

There were villages that were totally dependent on the baron's administration. These included Rishon le-Zion, Zichron Ya'acov, Rosh Pina, Ekron and others, which the baron founded himself. And there were settlements that were partially dependent on him, villages where some of the settlers were supported by him, like Petah Tikva or Hadera, where the settlers succeeded, with the baron's help, in draining the malarial, mosquito-breeding marshes.

The PICA villages were another type of settlement. They were smaller, based on field crops and had a more modest life style. As is commonly known, they played an important part in the absorption of the Second Aliyah, which we will discuss later. There were also workers' settlements, such as Ein Zeitim, Be'er Tuvia and Menahemiyah.

There were, of course, very great economic differences between the different types, between the Galilee and the coastal plain, between workers' settlements and the older, well-established villages. These differences were expressed in the outward appearance of the settlements, in the way of life, in dress, in the education of the children, and of their fate. It should be understood that very many of the children of the wealthier, more cultured villages, those strongly affected by the French spirit, left the country and scattered to the ends of the earth. They can be found in Europe, Australia, Africa, and even in New York.

Things reached the point that, when Arthur Ruppin visited the country in 1907 as an envoy of the Zionist Federation, he wrote in his report that only one thing could save these settlements, a transfusion of new, young blood. There was one man who thought of this before him. That was Menachem Ussishkin, who tried to found a new Bilu organization, a sort of semi-military organization of young people who would volunteer to work in the settlements for a specified period.

From this point of view, the situation in the other settlements was different, and perhaps better. But we should remember that the First Aliyah was not only an enterprise directed from the start toward settlement on the land. At this time there was also another, urban society, outside the villages, which had grown up and developed more or less independently, and to which the First Aliyah also supplied fresh blood.

At the end of the nineteenth century and the beginning of the twentieth, following the First Aliyah, the Jewish community grew to 50,000; 28,000 of these in Jerusalem. The Jerusalem Jewish population consisted of 15,000 Ashkenazim and 13,000 Sephardim or immigrants from other countries in Asia and Africa. 6,000 Jews lived in Safed, 5,000 in Jaffa, 1,400 in Haifa and more than 3,000 in Tiberias.

In these towns, the trend towards productivization was growing ever stronger. Crafts developed and there were even signs of light industry. About 45% of the Jews of Jerusalem supported themselves by labor, crafts, or trade. There was also a very important development in the field of Hebrew education, which grew in strength and began to compete with the influence of French and German culture. The Hebrew language spread mainly in the settlements, but also in the towns. The enterprise of Ben Yehuda, that lonely fighter for the Hebrew language, grew and gathered strength. Hebrew became an instrument of communication between the communities. The mixed families which arose as a result of marriages between people from Europe and natives of

38

Africa or Asia were the ones that used Hebrew, and this gave the language a very important role, far beyond the purely cultural sphere. Hebrew journalism also developed, particularly that of Ben Yehuda. Papers like *Hashkafah*, *Hatzvi* and *Ha'or* spread the word for the Yishuv, both among its members and abroad.

In 1903 an attempt was made to create a communal leadership for the Yishuv in Eretz Israel. Here we come up against a certain paradox. The Yishuv, founded as a result of nationalist ambitions, was incapable of establishing from among its ranks a common leadership to direct it, to organize it, to gather its problems together and to present them in a concise form to those to whom they should be presented.

The idea of such a leadership was proposed by Menachem Ussishkin, the Eastern European Zionist leader who was active in many fields, one of the most prominent figures of the Zionist Congress, the head of Hovevei Zion, and an opponent of Herzl. It was he who suggested the idea of the new Bilu, which should reflect his activist nature. Menachem Ussishkin initiated the first conference of representatives of the entire Yishuv in order to create for itself a common elected representation. The conference met in 1903 in Zichron Ya'acov, accompanied by very great excitement, flags, bands, horseback riders, excited speeches, and very good intentions. But it proved extremely difficult to put these intentions into practice. This was because the society was split and because, in reality, there were local organizations, regional organizations and various kinds of philanthropic organizations, all of which were stronger than the common organization founded by Ussishkin. Village committees; the associations that operated in Eretz Israel, like PICA; the Alliance administration and its educational enterprise; and even the workers' committees; all had their own particular power. The common interest was of less importance in their eyes. For them, the main thing was the solution of limited local problems. Moreover, the organization had no power and no authority to impose its will upon them.

What was the inheritance left by the First Aliyah to the immigration waves that followed? Of course, it laid the foundations

39

for the new Jewish society in Eretz Israel. It also laid the foundations both for the rural settlements and for settlement in the towns, since one cannot imagine the totality of Jewish settlement without its urban society. This urban society, whether consciously or not, whether directly or indirectly, served as a supportive hinterland for the settlement in villages. The First Aliyah bequeathed to the period that followed Hebrew education, urban settlement, crafts and light industry. It also bequeathed experience of the difficulties of life in Eretz Israel — experience in all fields, including labor, security and defense.

The First Aliyah also handed down problems created in its time, which it could not solve itself, or perhaps had not even intended to solve, and the later waves of immigration were forced to grapple with them.

One of these was the problem of non-Jewish labor in the settlements, which became more and more common in the period that followed. This problem led to a historical phenomenon which we shall discuss later — the struggle for the conquest of Hebrew labor. This struggle accompanied the Jewish Yishuv from the time of the Second Aliyah almost until the establishment of the State.

It is necessary to understand that in the settlements, mainly the large ones and in particular those founded in the second wave of the First Aliyah such as Rehovot, there were hundreds of Jewish laborers who supported themselves by working for the farmers. In some years, numbers of laborers attempted to organize themselves so as to help to improve their lives, with ventures such as cooperative kitchens, cultural clubs, communal living, and even some organizations for defense. The start of the defense organizations was in Rehovot in the 1890's, in the associations of "the Ten," or "the Brothers," which were organized as a sort of secret society for the defence of the villages.

But these laborers did not intend to remain as hired hands. They wanted to become settlers, or to "farmerize" themselves, in the language of that time. They tried to save their money to buy land. Public bodies also bought land and founded settlements for them. These were settlements like Be'er Tuvia and Ein Zeitim. But their organization faced a crisis situation. There was a shortage of work in the villages as a result of the new economics of PICA, and some Jewish laborers found a solution to the employment problem by settling in Galilee. But there were laborers whose only solution was to leave the country, and in more than a few cases they were assisted in doing so by the PICA officials.

The settlement movement needed shaking up; it needed the infusion of fresh blood, new concepts, a new direction. It would appear that, at the beginning of the twentieth century, the First Aliyah had reached its limit as the national enterprise. New forces were needed to make it march forward. We have already suggested that both Ussishkin and Ruppin, who visited the country at the beginning of the century, understood that the enterprise could be saved from its rigidity and atrophy in the national sense, in their terms, only by a new social force, which would give it a stimulus and put it back on a renewed national path.

V.

The Period of The Second Aliyah

In 1904, immigrants of a different kind began to come to Eretz Israel. A new type of immigrant arrived, bringing with him the dream, the legend, and the great plans of the Zionist Utopia. Thus, in effect, began the Second Aliyah, which started in 1904 and ended with the outbreak of the First World War in 1914. But before discussing and analyzing this new and revolutionary phenomenon, which was embodied in the young people of the Second Aliyah, we must deal with the character of the period as a whole.

The second event closest to it in time was the "Uganda conflict," The events of those years were what impelled many of these immigrants to come to Eretz Israel. Here we refer to the pogrom at Kishinev, which sent a great shock wave through the Jewish public, especially the young. It shocked them, not only because of the cruelty involved, but because of the lack of reaction from the Jews facing this cruelty. At that time, many went about weighed down by a great sense of humiliation, and for many aliyah was a reaction to that humiliation.

The second event closest to it in time was the "Uganda conflict," which nearly split the Zionist Federation. For many of the Zionists of Eastern Europe and Russia, even the fact that this was proposed was a betrayal of the essence of the Zionist ideal. Following this came the death of Herzl in 1904, which also greatly shocked the Zionist movement, which had suddenly lost its leader. Even when it opposed his leadership, even when it rebelled against him, even

42

when the movement was almost split, Russian Jewry saw Herzl as its leader, almost as the King Messiah.

In addition to these, there was another event, which took place outside the Jewish realm, but which had a great influence on the Jews — thr Russian revolution of 1905, the revolution with liberal aims which failed. The failure of this revolution; the blow inflicted on the Jews by the different pogroms at the time of the revolution; and the Jewish reaction toward self defense, that is the organizing for self defense that began within the Jewish Pale of Settlement; all these prompted many people to migrate to Eretz Israel.

These events marked the beginning of the period. Its end was far more clear; it was closed by the First World War, not only because immigration was halted during the war, but also because at the end of this period political events took place of revolutionary significance for the history of Zionism and of the Jewish people: the conquest of Eretz Israel by the British and the Balfour Declaration.

The Second Aliyah was numerically similar to the First Aliyah. In these ten years there were between twenty and thirty thousand Jewish immigrants. Like the First Aliyah, the Second was also marked by both revolutionary tendencies and by signs of continuity. This aliyah showed continuity in its way of life and many of its aims, in which it followed in the footsteps of both the Old and the New Yishuvs. But the Second Aliyah had certain revolutionary tendencies, which were displayed by the groups of young people from which grew up the Workers' Movement. We shall dedicate a separate chapter to this movement. It must be emphasized that these young people were a minority among the immigrants of the Second Aliyah, while the vast majority of the immigrants who came at that time were from the middle class. The latter preferred to live in the Jewish urban communities and not in the agricultural settlements. Some joined the Old Yishuv, some the New, and a few went to the villages. As a result of both this immigration and of natural increase, the Jewish population of Eretz Israel continued to grow. During this decade, the population increased from 50,000 to 85,000. At the end of the period about 12,000 of them lived in the settlements.

According to estimates, in 1914 about half the Jewish population belonged to the New Yishuv, and about half, those who were connected with "kolels" (groups from one country or district) and received Halukah, were members of the Old Yishuv.

The number of Jews in Jaffa reached 10,000. In Haifa it also rose, to 3,000. The Jewish population of Jerusalem reached 45,000, of whom 30,000 belonged to the Old Yishuv, according to the criterion of receiving Halukah.

In addition to the traditional urban communities, if we can call them that, it was in this period that the foundation stone was laid for the first Hebrew city, Tel Aviv. This was founded in 1909 by the Ahuzat Bayit association, which built the Neve Zedek quarter. In the towns themselves there were significant and important developments in the fields of trade, crafts and even banking, which began to develop at this time.

The towns also began to develop a stratum of wage earners, mostly from the Old Yishuv, including print workers and other craftsmen. Agriculture also continued to establish itself. We have already stated that, following the management transfer from the baron's administration to that of PICA, and despite the latter's harsh economic policy and frugality towards the farmers, in the end the new policy benefited them. It gradually transferred responsibility for managing the farms and the enterprises from the administration to the farmers. The best example is the creation of the cooperative associations of wine-growers. In 1906 the wineries were in practice turned over to these associations' independent management.

The PICA officials also initiated the introduction of new branches of orchard cultivation in the villages. Most importantly, they renewed the growing of oranges, and this later became the principal export sector and brought economic prosperity to many of the settlements of the First Aliyah.

At the same time, a number of companies were founded for managing orchards. They were in a way equitable companies of Zionists, who invested their money and entrusted the management of the orchards to those responsible locally, these being the various estates. The foundation of new settlements in Lower Galilee by PICA has already been mentioned. These settlements were based on field crops, with a standard of living appropriate to conditions in Eretz Israel and similar to that of the Arab peasants. These were Sejera, Kfar Tabor and Yavniel. Another phenomenon at this time, which should be stressed, is the appearance in the villages of Jewish workers from the Yemen.

The aliyah from the Yemen to Eretz Israel in the period of the Second Aliyah was the continuation of immigration by Yemenite Jews in the First Aliyah period, in 1882. These Jews came to the settlements, to a large degree through the initiative of the prominent Second Aliyah figure, Yavnieli, who travelled to Yemen and encouraged them to emigrate. They suffered severe hardships in the settlements. They were culturally alienated from their environment, both that of the farmers and that of the laborers. They had families and were forced to support them on the pay of a daily laborer, which was sometimes less than that of a single man of Ashkenazi origin.

This phenomenon, which, it is true, can be explained by the cultural gap and the limited means available to both the farmers and the workers' organizations, was not to the credit of either the settlements or the Workers' Movement, which despite the objective alienation between it and the Yemenite laborers, did not do enough to absorb them. This was one of the tragedies that accompanied the building enterprise from the beginning to the present day.

Another development, very important both in its own day and for the future, was the progress made in Hebrew education. New education, that is education outside the "heder" (traditional religious primary school), received important assistance from the Alliance Israelite Universelle and also from the Ezra Society founded by German Jews. This education was conducted by teachers who regarded their work as a pioneering enterprise, as a national alternative to both the traditional "heder" education and to that of the missions.

The most important achievement of Hebrew education was in the settlements. It can be said that from 1908 onwards, Hebrew was the predominant language for instruction in the village schools. On the other hand, the situation in the towns was far more complicated and the position of Hebrew, which had to compete there with French and German, was far more difficult. Thus the struggle to establish Hebrew education gradually became a sort of national mission. As a result of this struggle, the Hebrew teachers acquired the position of national leaders. A cultural elite was created of teachers, who had as their life's goal the implanting of Hebrew and Hebrew education.

The teachers were consistent in their methods. They established programs for qualifying teachers and also founded colleges for training them. Gradually, the status of Hebrew improved, particularly in the towns. This process came into conflict with earlier, non-Hebrew trends, as in the famous 1913 "Language War," which was concerned with the question of the language of instruction in the technical high school in Haifa, the present-day Technion.

The Ezra Society of German Jews, which, as mentioned, did a great deal to establish modern education in this country, both by its foundation of a teachers' college and by the setting up of a school for commerce and for horticulture, insisted on teaching in German as well as Hebrew. The Hebrew teachers accepted this as a fact of life, but were not happy about it and were not always resigned to it. They nevertheless accepted it in practice. In 1913, though, Ezra tried to create a completely new fact. Its plan was to build a technical high school alongside the Reali school in Haifa. In 1913 the board of directors of Ezra decided that scientific and technological studies should be conducted in German. This decision was logical for both scientific and pedagogic reasons, as the text books were written in German. But this scientific and pedagogic logic clashed with national aspirations. A general rebellion broke out both in the Zionist movement and in the Jewish Yishuv, among intellectuals like Ahad Ha'am, among the teachers and even among the workers, who were apparently remote from intellectual affairs, but who adopted this cause.

The establishment of the Hebrew language in this high school, the future Technion, became a matter of principle. It was accompanied by motifs that were, to some extent, foreign to the language controversy itself, but which were not entirely inappropriate. The directorate of Ezra was accused of assimilationist tendencies, which was not all that far from the truth, despite the fact that the society did a great deal to educate Jews. It was accused of political aims, in that the introduction of the German language served the political interest of its native land, Germany. There was a certain amount of truth in these accusations. But basically it was a struggle of the Jewish community, headed by the teachers — particularly the teachers' federation, which was founded in 1903 and was the first professional trade union in the country — on behalf of the Hebrew language and, through it, the national interest.

In the end, the victory of Hebrew was also interpreted as a victory for the national interest. As a result of the outcome of this struggle, Hebrew education gained a very great deal. In a paradoxical way this crisis is praiseworthy (and we shall return to it later in the discussion), because it was precisely from it that a constructive outcome resulted. Due to this conflict, an independent Hebrew education network was set up under the aegis of a public education committee, founded during the period of the struggle. The management of this committee was largely Zionist. This period, in fact, saw the beginnings of Hebrew education under the patronage of the Zionist movement. It continued to develop at a later period.

To sum up, the constructive trends which had begun in the First Aliyah continued in the Second, such as laying the foundation for Jewish settlement and its development, the building of a new urban Jewish society, the development of Hebrew education, and the modernization of the economic system in the fields of commerce and banking. But the unique quality of the Second Aliyah was not in its continuity, but in its trends toward change. It was these that led to a historic turning point in the settlement enterprise in this country and eventually also to a revolution in national concepts. These trends toward change brought to the forefront of Zionist vision and the Jewish community in Eretz Israel, especially in the field of building activity, new forces, different from all those that had preceded them.

It should be noted that, at the beginning of the Second Aliyah, a new trend in the activities of the Zionist institutions began to be apparent. It must be understood that, with the death of Herzl, an era in the history of the Zionist Federation had come to an end and a new era had begun. The period that had ended was one of diplomatic storm and stress, of the belief that it was possible to obtain for the Jewish people, through diplomatic means, through the aspiration for an agreement with the powers, a charter, a kind of memorandum of consent between a great power and the Jewish people, which would make possible mass settlement in Eretz Israel.

With the death of Herzl, this idea vanished. It did not fail because of the death of Herzl. Its failure was to be expected even during his lifetime. The new era that began was one of practical Zionism, or "synthetic Zionism," which combined political aims with practical aims — that is settlement in Eretz Israel. On the other hand, the possibilities for political action were few and grew less with the passage of time. Following the revolution of the Young Turks in 1908, it quickly became clear that, despite the hopes placed in these young revolutionaries, they had became anti-Zionist, not out of hatred for Zionism or Jews, but because they were opposed to all national organizations, particularly to the penetration of modern nationalist ideas imported from the West to the East. Since the opportunities for political activity were minimal, the principal effort was turned to practical action. And indeed from 1907 onwards, the Zionist Federation entered with new strength, which continued to grow in the following decades, into practical activity in Eretz Israel. We have already pointed out that in the First Aliyah an attempt was made by the Hovevei Zion to assist in settlement, and that they even founded a village — the Bilu village of Gedera. But through short-sightedness and lack of means their role ended there.

In the second wave of the First Aliyah, in the period of Tyomkin, an attempt was made to buy large contiguous tracts of land, but it failed. There was nothing completely new in this from the point of view of public initiative. The innovation was that from now on the public initiative became consistent and influenced the settlement enterprise to an ever-increasing extent. This initiative was associated with the name of one man, Arthur Ruppin, who was sent to Eretz Israel on behalf of the Zionist Federation, and who founded the "Palestine Office." Ruppin was a young Jewish sociologist of German origin, from a middle-class family, who was converted to Zionism and decided to devote his time and his life to practical Zionism. He headed this enterprise for many years and set his seal on it until the foundation of the State. Ruppin was the father of the settlement enterprise of the Second Aliyah. Just as Rothschild is considered the "Father of the Yishuv," so can Ruppin be considered the "Father of the Workers."

VI.

The Beginning of The Workers' Movement

Dr. Arthur Ruppin headed the Zionist movement's settlement enterprise in Eretz Israel. He wanted, first and foremost, to concentrate the national initiative on land acquisition through the channels of the Jewish National Fund, and was also the initiator of the establishment of blocks of Jewish settlement and the creation of territorial continuity between them, principally the link between Galilee and Judea and Samaria.

Ruppin made great efforts to assist the foundation of urban neighborhoods, such as Neve Zedek (which later grew into Tel Aviv), and the Hadar HaCarmel quarter in Haifa. It was he who put forward a plan for assisting idealistic young people who came to Eretz Israel and wanted to become farmers. He did this not in order to help unemployed young people who needed an income, or young people who needed some sort of constructive solution to be found for them, but primarily because he was aware that it was precisely these young people who would advance the realization of Zionism in the future. Thus Ruppin became the "Father of the Workers."

Who were these young people who came to Eretz Israel? Nearly all of them were from middle class families. They came from the Pale of Settlement in Russia, where they had no definite occupation, no trade, no formal education. The proportion of students among them was very small, but nearly all of them had some informal education, either the traditional education of heder and yeshiva, or general secular education. They brought to Eretz Israel a very

50

important stock of principles, values and attitudes prevalent in Russia at that time. As has been said, there were not many of them, even in relation to the numbers of that time. Generally there were fewer than a thousand of them in the settlements, and emigration from the country affected this group more than others.

But, despite being a numerical minority, or perhaps because of it, they laid the foundations for the Workers' Movement in Eretz Israel, as an organization with national and social values, that developed its own instruments for putting those values into practice. It is clear therefore, that, even in the early stages, this movement was different from other workers' movements elsewhere in the world. It did not grow from the labor heritage, from cultural inertia, from the natural cultural development through which farmers move to the towns and enter employment in factories together with craftsmen impoverished or displaced by the growth of industry. This workers' movement of the Second Aliyah was founded on the principle of choice.

We emphasize the principle of choice, because it had a triple significance. First of all, these young people chose Eretz Israel and not the U.S.A., despite the fact that at that time America's gates stood open to immigration. Other alternative possibilities for immigration were also available to them, as they were for their comrades and brothers.

Their second choice was in their decision to stay in Eretz Israel, although among them the percentage who emigrated from the country was the highest. The reality of Eretz Israel served as a kind of selective factor. Those who remained did so basically because they wanted to stay. Moreover, most of them came from the Jewish bourgeoisie and their parents' homes were open to them economically as well.

Finally, they chose to belong to the Workers' Movement. They were a group with theories, a band for whom theories had practical significance. Their theories were synthetic, based on a combination of socialism and nationalism on the one hand, and idealism and nationalism on the other. There were differences between them. They founded parties which argued and fought between themselves.

There was the non-socialist "HaPo'el HaTza'ir" (Young Worker) party, founded in 1905. There was the socialist "Po'alei Zion" (Workers of Zion) party, founded in 1906. There was also a non-party group, which was said, perhaps not in jest, to be the non-party party. There were differences between them, but there were also common basic features. From now on we will stress what was common to them rather than their differences.

The first common basic feature can be defined as practical national activism, bearing a personal significance. The duty of creation of a nation was imposed on every individual and the assumption of that burden depended on each one's personal decision. Another basic feature common to them all, despite the ideological differences between them, was their mission as a movement or as a class. These young people were, as mentioned, a very small group; they were few in numbers, even according to the ideas of the time; there were never more than a few hundred of them in the settlements at any given time because of the continued turnover. People came and went. People came, saw, tried to work, failed in their work, were broken and left. Despite their poverty and despite their small numbers, they carried with them a world-embracing national mission. They were convinced that Zionism could not exist without the workers. There were those who said that Zionism could not exist without a workers' party; and those who said, "not without the working public;" and the socialists, who said, "not without the working class." But common to them all was the idea and the sense that history had in a way chosen these workers, these laborers, to be its standard bearers, and that they were the ones who should lead the Zionist movement and the Jewish people to their national goal in Eretz Israel. This mission was a fusion of national aspirations and social values, at the center of which stood a just and beautiful working society.

There was something Utopian in these theories, something of a dream, something of a craving for a kind of completeness — one that was not always agreed upon among them and moreover was not clear to different sections within them. But if they had been more Utopian, it is doubtful whether they would have been able to stamp their impression on history. They were more than merely Utopian dreamers: they were practical people. This was what made them create a kind of synthesis, a kind of combination of Utopianism and practicality. And so they turned from collaborators into partners, and finally into leaders in the national building enterprise.

Just as they created a combination of Utopianism and action, so they managed to blend the general interest with the wishes and aspirations of the individual. The achievement of the national goal was for them also the fulfillment of individual longings. At this point of achievement, the fusion between individual yearnings and the national will was created. This was the pioneer spirit which sprang from the Second Aliyah. It continued into later periods, in the 'twenties and 'thirties, and until the establishment of the State. The youth movement of those born in the country associated itself with this public. In this way the founders of the Eretz Israel labor movement, and afterwards also their disciples, put their stamp on the history of the Jewish community in Eretz Israel.

Our discussion, though, will concentrate on the practical side of their activities. First of all, they wanted to conquer Hebrew labor. We should remember that at the end of the First Aliyah the awareness was growing that a public and national effort was needed to free the settlements from non-Jewish labor, which in the eyes of many of the leaders was taboo. Therefore it was suggested that young people should be recruited for this task. We have mentioned Ussishkin, and Dr. Ruppin and his impressions on his first visit to Eretz Israel in 1907. The young people who came to the country, came with the desire to redeem the settlements from the shame of non-Jewish labor. It was considered shameful, because it was seen as one of the plagues of the national enterprise. They were aware that a national society cannot be built by the labor of foreigners. A national society must be built by members of that nation. In a paradoxical way, they favored the exploitation of Jews by Jews, rather than that of Arabs by Jews. On this point it is worth mentioning that in the early period, at the beginning of the century, they had already warned against an intensification of the Jewish-

Arab conflict by the creation of class tensions between the farmers and the Arab laborers.

But the distance between aspiration and reality was great. In their longing for Hebrew labor in the settlements, they came up against a harsh and resistant reality. There were many objective obstacles, which were very difficult to overcome. It should be understood that these young people came into an immediate confrontation with the existing society, that of the farmers. This confrontation had a number of dimensions. It was a conflict between two generations. It was an antagonism between rebellious young people, the bearers of various kinds of belief in redemption, socialists and non-socialists, and a traditional society which was becoming increasingly bourgeois. In some settlements, there was also a cultural conflict between these young people of the Second Aliyah — who were natives of Russia and who brought with them in their knapsacks Russian literature, Tolstoy, Dostoevsky, the theories of Russian socialism, and even a measure of Russian anarchism — and the previous Russian immigrants, who were from this point of view provincials. Particularly alien to them was the spiritual world of the natives of the land, born in the villages of Zichron Ya'acov, Petah Tikva or Rishon le-Zion. Against this background tension mounted between the two groups of young people, who were so different from each other.

There was also a confrontation between two societies, one secular and the other devout supporters of tradition, both in maintaining a positive attitude toward religion, and in their attitude toward the institution of the family. The farmers found morally offensive the behavior of these young people, particularly the women, who left home and came to live in the villages, carrying on a kind of communal life. The farmers strove to keep their children, particularly their daughters, away from these "dissolute" groups. As a result, the gulf between the two societies grew even wider. Evidence for this gulf lies in the limited number of marriages between the farmers' sons or daughters and the workers, male or female.

The economic factor also contributed greatly to this tension.

54

We are speaking here of the PICA period, the time at which the farmer had to prove the profitability of his farm in order to make a living. Viability became an economic problem of the first order. From the farmers' point of view Arab labor was cheaper, and, in many branches of agriculture, also more efficient and more convenient. The wage of an Arab laborer was about 40% lower than that of a Jewish one. The Arab laborer was both more expert in the work and physically stronger as well. He was not rebellious, he had not come to harass the farmers, to show them new ways, or to preach morality at them. He worked and obeyed their orders.

The young people, on the other hand, were not prepared to do this. They were quite arrogant toward the farmers, as regards both nationalism and culture. In this struggle, the farmers represented tradition and the existing socio-cultural and economic situation. The young represented, in their opinion, the national interest, the Zionist revolution, and social change.

In the first stage, the conflict between the two groups focused on the question of Hebrew labor. The young workers saw in this struggle the essence of their national and cultural aspirations, but this struggle failed. The young did not succeed in penetrating the villages, they did not succeed in making themselves an alternative to the Arab laborers. At the end of the period there arose an outcry that the transition to an orchard economy had resulted in a process of proletarianization among the Arabs, but not the Jews. The number of Arab laborers continued to grow. In certain settlements it reached thousands in the harvest season, and the number of Jewish laborers kept declining. The Jewish laborers did not succeed in breaking through the wall of cultural alienation and economic interest.

But history sometimes moves in mysterious ways that can be strange and even paradoxical, leading to the ends it has laid down; for from this failure, this crisis, sprang the solution that bore within it the seeds of what would become one of the most revolutionary enterprises of the Jewish settlement movement in Eretz Israel — communal settlement. But even though the failure in the struggle for Hebrew labor constituted a factor that prompted and stimulated the search for new ways and means, it was not the factor that directed the members of the Second Aliyah to the idea of communal settlement. They came to that from their nationalist and collectivist world view and on the basis of the ideas that they had acquired through the years.

The idea of communal settlement began with the scheme of a Jewish economist and sociologist of Utopian tendencies, Franz Oppenheimer, who was converted to Zionism. At the beginning of the century he suggested to the Zionist Federation that it should set up cooperative settlements for the laborers, where they could work in collaboration and be paid for their labors, gradually equip themselves for work on the land, and finally aim at managing independent farms. These cooperative farms would be run, according to this plan, by administrators, principally agronomists, appointed by the Zionist movement.

When this suggestion was put to the young people of the Second Aliyah, they were skeptical. Many of them had reservations, some, such as HaPo'el HaTza'ir, because they had still not renounced the idea of Hebrew labor in the settlements. Others saw this plan as a betrayal of the class struggle in that, instead of fighting the class war against the farmers in the villages, they would be going to make themselves the bourgeoisie in their own settlements.

In 1909, after much debate, it was again, in a paradoxical way, the socialists who were the first to agree to Oppenheimer's plan. They saw in it a way of strengthening the working class and of enabling Jewish workers to be absorbed in settlement. This led to the experiment of Merhaviah, the cooperative settlement founded according to the Oppenheimer plan, which did not succeed. It failed because disputes arose between the administration, appointed by institutions of the Zionist movement, and the workers. On the other hand, these ideas were accepted by other groups; groups who worked in the Galilee, and they put forward the idea of an independent workers' settlement. These were the groups that in 1910 founded Degania, the cornerstone of the cooperative settlement project. Degania also was founded as a result of a combination of aims: Ruppin's aim to give more and more independence to the workers on the one hand, and the workers' desire to achieve independent status; independence from the farmers on the one hand and from the supervisors on the other. Degania also arose from the Utopian longings of many of the workers, particularly those of Josef Bussel, the spiritual leader of the group that founded it, to establish communal, communist settlements, which should serve as instruments for national realization.

Apart from its settlement activity, the crowning achievement of which was Degania — the model for future such settlements — this movement's activity expressed itself in other fields as well, principally that of defense. It was this movement and this public from which the "HaShomer" (Watchman) organization sprang up. This organization attempted to take upon itself the responsibility for the national defense of the Jewish community in Eretz Israel. There was in this some sort of continuity of the effort to conquer both labor and the land, and the continuation of the tendency to give the workers a central place in the formation of a new Yishuv. What happened in the Second Aliyah, as a result of the struggle to work the land, from the beginnings of communal labor, and the foundation of HaShomer as a defense arm (from which the Israel Defense Forces eventually developed), and what was created at that time, gave the working class, for the first time in the Jews' long history, a critical role in the process of development and a decisive position in determining the national destiny of the people.

It should also be noted that the Second Aliyah laid down the basis for the Yishuv's political system. The political parties of HaPo'el HaTza'ir and Po'alei Zion were founded in that period. The foundations were also laid for the trade union, from which, in a strange metamorphosis, evolved the General Histadrut (Trade Union Federation), with all its importance for the national enterprise.

To sum up the period, it can be said that the practical achievements of the Second Aliyah period, especially among the working public, were not great; in fact, they were meager. Numerically, this enterprise was not very significant. But qualitatively, considering its advances in cooperative settlement, in defense, in the formulation of a world view and the emergence of a group of leaders such as Ben Gurion, Berl Katznelson, Tabenkin, Ben Zvi, Sprintzak and others, who later became leaders of the Yishuv and of the nation, considering all these precedents, this aliyah served as a springboard for future change.

VII.

The Period of
The Third Aliyah

At the end of the discussion of the Second Aliyah, we argued that the First World War made a sharp division between two periods in the history of Zionist construction. And indeed at the end of the war a new period began in the history of Zionism. The Balfour Declaration, granted to the Zionist movement by Great Britain — one of the great powers of the time — changed the status of the movement, both in the international arena and among the Jewish people. This declaration gave the Jews international recognition of their right to return to Eretz Israel. It did not give them the right to all of Eretz Israel, but it gave them the right to build a national home in Eretz Israel. Thus a great power recognized not only Jewish aspirations to return to Eretz Israel, but also Jewish nationalism, on which doubts had been cast in an earlier period.

The declaration was later ratified by the League of Nations. Thus the recognition of Jewish nationalism was awarded an international seal of approval. As a result of the conquest of Eretz Israel by Great Britain, the status of Zionism underwent a substantial change. While Turkey never recognized the right to organize on a national basis, Great Britain, both in its support for the Arab national movement in all the countries surrounding Eretz Israel, and in its granting of the Balfour Declaration, in effect acknowledged the rights of both the national movements.

From this time onwards, Jewish nationalism was no longer an underground affair, but an official one, recognized by the governing power in Eretz Israel, and internationally approved. The Zionist Federation was also recognized by the British government and was designated in the text of the mandate under which Eretz Israel was awarded to Great Britain by the League of Nations as representing the interests of the Jewish people. It should be stressed that the Balfour Declaration was given not to the Zionist movement, but to the Jewish people. The Zionist movement nevertheless became the representative of the nation's interests in Eretz Israel.

An additional line of political development in this period should also be stressed. The first signs of violent conflict between Jews and Arabs can be traced to the beginning of the 1920's. Arab opposition to Jewish settlement in Eretz Israel, the first hints of which were noticeable at the time of the First Aliyah, intensified. This opposition became rather more extreme during the Second Aliyah, in 1908, following the revolution of the Young Turks, and acquired its ideological dimension at that time. The fear of Jewish control of Eretz Israel had existed earlier, but it reached its violent stage at the beginning of the 1920's. The disturbances in Jerusalem in 1920 and in Jaffa in 1921 clearly foretold what the future held in store: almost unavoidable, violent, armed conflict between the two national movements.

As regards aliyah itself, here too signs of continuity and signs of change were visible in the period from 1917 to 1923. At this time change was more noticeable than continuity. This, the Third Aliyah, comprised about 36,000 immigrants. This in itself bears witness to great negligence on the part of the Jewish people, for in those years mass immigration was still possible. Even when certain restrictions were imposed on Jewish immigration to Eretz Israel, it was still possible for the middle class to come. But the people of Israel, when they were asked, "where are you?" did not respond.

Of the 36,000 that did come, most were young. We shall say more about them later. As a result of this aliyah and of natural increase, at the end of the period, in 1924, the Yishuv numbered 85,000 Jews. It should be noted that the Jewish population of Eretz Israel had fallen considerably during the First World War, as a result of expulsion and of the mortality rate caused by disease. Thus by 1924 the Yishuv had merely attained its size before the First World War.

As had happened before, most of this aliyah streamed into the towns. The New Yishuv grew considerably at this time. In Jaffa, for example, which had had 6,000 Jews before the war, the Jewish population reached 20,000 by the end of the period. Nearly all of these lived in the new city of Tel Aviv.

The change, as suggested, was basic, and was revolutionary from many different points of view. It took place in many different spheres, first of all, in the outer sphere, that of the Zionist movement. That movement, under the leadership of Chaim Weizmann, took on a new image. It became the representative of the Jewish people when it took upon itself full representation of the Jews politically, culturally and economically. In addition, at the same time the Zionist movement became an active factor in constructive Zionism. Its role in construction, which, as suggested, began in the Second Aliyah, became more and more significant.

The second sphere, the inner one, was that of the institutions of the autonomous, national Jewish leadership in Eretz Israel. Immediately after the conquest or, depending on one's point of view, the liberation of the country by the British, an attempt was made to create autonomous institutions for the Jewish community in Eretz Israel. In long drawn out negotiations and disputes between the different sections: between the religious and secular, where the controversy was over women's right to vote; between the Workers' Movement and the farmers; with reservations by some leaders and exaggerated claims by others; and despite the tensions — which also had an ethnic element — in the end a framework for Jewish autonomy in Eretz Israel was established — Knesset Israel. This represented the Jewish community of Eretz Israel before the British authorities and, to a degree, inside the Zionist movement as well. In this it realized the dream of Ussishkin in 1903, in the first days of the First Aliyah. Knesset Israel, though, did not represent *all* the Jews of Eretz Israel, because, when it was finally decided to give the vote to women, ultra-orthodox groups resigned from it. But the great majority of the Yishuv belonged to this voluntary, autonomous body. In 1927 the organization received official recognition from the Mandate government.

The third sphere, the central one, was that of the Histadrut, the political and social framework of the Workers' Movement. The Histadrut served as an all-inclusive workers' organization. It was all-inclusive in that it included all occupations, not only agricultural laborers as in the Second Aliyah, including workers from both the country and the town and the intelligentsia; anyone, in fact, who worked by his own efforts and did not exploit the labor of others. The organization was also inclusive in another sense, in the functions it had to fill. It was founded not only as a trade union, but as an organization with wider roles to play, in settlement, in defense, in culture and in immigration. From the start, the Histadrut was intended as an organization that would undertake national tasks, as, for example, the foundation of the underground "Haganah" (Defense) organization, to guard the security of the entire Yishuv. It also wished to build a different Jewish society from the foundations up.

As had already happened with the creation of the national institutions of the Yishuv's autonomous body, Knesset Israel, the creation of the Histadrut was also accompanied by internal tensions and power struggles. The historic role of the Histadrut should be evaluated against the background of these conflicts, and we can thus appreciate all the more how this organization nevertheless succeeded in leading the Yishuv and the Zionist movement toward their national goals. Without the Histadrut and the social forces that organized within it, the national fate of the Histadrut and the social character of the Yishuv in Eretz Israel would undoubtedly have been different.

As regards the subject of these chapters — the constructive activity of the Zionist enterprise — two of the these spheres concern us, the first, the outer sphere, that is the Zionist movement; and the last, the inner one, the one in the center, the Histadrut.

At the beginning of the 1920's, after the Balfour Declaration, the Zionist movement was locked in a fierce dispute between two conceptions of Zionism. The two leading Jewish personalities of that time represented these two conceptions. On one side was Chaim Weizmann, whose name was linked with the Balfour Declaration, and who, even before he was elected to the presidency of the Zionist Federation, was in fact the leader of the movement. On the other side was Louis Brandeis, who was perhaps the most famous of all Jews, both among his own people and among the Gentiles. He was a Justice of the Supreme Court of the U.S.A., close to the President, a man who came to Zionism by a route that was tortuous, strange and not always intelligible, and became a supporter of the idea of constructive Zionism.

Brandeis' conception of Zionism was different from that of Weizmann. Weizmann believed that, after the Balfour Declaration, the Zionist movement had to represent the interests of the Jewish people, both to the British government in Eretz Israel, and in the Diaspora. The role of the Zionist movement, in his view, was to concentrate within it all the problems of the Jewish people and to guide the people in a certain direction. Brandeis, however, thought differently. He opposed the centralist view of Weizmann. In his opinion, the political struggle had ended with the Balfour Declaration and the British Mandate over Eretz Israel. Henceforth the Zionist Federation had no further political function and its only duty was to help people to settle in Eretz Israel. But even this assistance in settlement should be decentralized. The Zionist Federation ought to agree to the decentralization of fund raising. Each national federation ought to take the initiative in aid for settlement. The Zionist Federation ought to turn to private initiators and encourage them to invest in Eretz Israel. It should raise funds for projects concerned with the infrastructure, like roads, marsh drainage, or education, but no more than that. Brandeis supported collective settlement and capitalist investment, but argued that things should arise from the spontaneous initiative of owners of capital and various groups, and that the Zionist Federation should limit its role in this matter.

In Weizmann's view this was heresy, and heresy not only against the essence of the constructive role of the Zionist movement. He

63

accused Brandeis of splitting, in his own way, the efforts of the Jewish people, and claimed that the background to his views was ideological; that he believed that there was no all-inclusive Jewish unity. According to Weizmann, Brandeis was prepared to recognize Jewish unity only in regard to its focus in Eretz Israel, whereas he believed that from the Zionist viewpoint Jewish unity was all-inclusive and world-embracing.

Behind the controversy between Weizmann and Brandeis lay the traditional conflict between western and eastern views of Zionism. By various means, not excluding political tactics and personal attacks, Weizmann succeeded in overcoming Brandeis' opposition. As a result, Brandeis and his important supporters, such as Justice Frankfurter and others, withdrew from active participation in the Zionist movement. The drive launched by Weizmann to raise enormous sums of money for the Keren Hayesod, for the development of settlements in Eretz Israel, was quite seriously harmed by Brandeis' withdrawal.

Nevertheless, one cannot maintain that, had Brandeis cooperated, the enterprise would have succeeded to the extent expected of it at the time. The initiators of the project hoped to collect 25,000,000 pounds sterling for its needs, but in fact collected only a small fraction of that sum. As a result, the means of the Zionist movement were fairly limited. During the 1920's and at the beginning of the 1930's, the Zionist movement was poor. Because its budgets were small and restricted, the movement was forced to determine priorities in investing national funds. As a result of the priorities established, its money was directed primarily toward settlement projects initiated by the movement. Thus, between 1920 and 1923, thirty one settlements were founded in Eretz Israel, six of which were established by PICA, twenty two by Zionist institutions, and the rest by private bodies. From that time onwards, the scales of new settlement formation tipped from those initiated by private individuals, or associations like PICA, toward those of the Zionist Federation.

The candidates for settlement by the Zionist Federation were primarily the young workers. As a result, most of the settlements founded and most of the funds invested were in the field of collective settlement. We shall return to this point, which bears witness to the pact formed between the Workers' Movement and the Zionist leadership headed by Chaim Weizmann. This pact, which arose at the beginning of the 1920's against a background of agreement in the field of construction, led to a political coalition in the Zionist Federation at the end of the decade.

In addition, the Federation also assisted the public economic enterprises of the Workers' Movement, such as Bank HaPo'alim, and the building company Solel Boneh. The Zionist Federation made great efforts to assist the workers in buying arms for underground activities, though it must be stressed that funds intended for defense purposes, like those used for the purchase of pistols and ammunition, were frequently transferred in a sort of private deal between Weizmann and Eliyahu Golomb and some of the Jewish contributors in England, principally the Rothschild family. On this basis of common action in the fields of settlement and defense, the personal connections between Chaim Weizmann and the leaders of the workers' Histadrut were strengthened.

We mentioned the pact between Weizmann and the Workers' Movement. This pact did not arise by accident. It was a pact between a liberal Zionist leader, who was not a socialist, who did not always have a favorable opinion of the workers and frequently complained of the troubles they caused him, and a movement of young people who were critical of Weizmann's leadership and occasionally suspicious of his intentions. This pact was not accidental; it was woven between people who were not naive in their reciprocal relationship, but it was founded out of Zionist need. Weizmann understood that if the Federation took the construction role upon itself, it would need to find people to put it into practice, and he found them, in his opinion, only among the workers.

From Weizmann's personal point of view, he found a kind of realization of the ideals of his youth in this meeting with the people of the Third Aliyah — the children of rich Jewish families, the students, or those who were ostensibly students — who knelt by the roadsides, breaking rocks. To him, the ideal was the idealistic

Jewish student, who dedicates himself to the cause of his people. Here Weizmann suddenly saw him before his eyes, and he gave expression to this feeling in his letters to his wife, where he was certainly not pretending.

Moreover, there was also a certain political consideration. Weizmann needed supporters in his struggle against Brandeis and, even though the political strength of the Workers' Movement in the Zionist movement, was meager at the time, the public and moral reverberations of its deeds were great, and that helped Weizmann.

On the other hand, the Workers' Movement quickly understood that if it wanted to be at the head of Zionist construction, it needed to acquire capital for its enterprise, and that capital could not come from its own resources. The Jewish workers in the Diaspora were not able, even if they wished, to contribute substantial funds to the Zionist enterprise. So, this capital could come only from the Jewish bourgeoisie, through the Zionist movement. The Workers' Movement neede the Zionist movement to support its enterprise.

In this way was formed the constructive pact between the Zionist leadership headed by Weizmann and the leaders of the Workers' Movement, despite the criticisms and the reciprocal complaints. At the end of the 'twenties, as mentioned, this pact would acquire a noticeable political dimension, both in the internal struggles of the Zionist movement, such as the rejection of the Revisionist opposition; and in the external struggles, in the relationship between the Zionist movement and the British government.

VIII.

The National Contribution of the Workers' Movement

We have emphasized the fact that Weizmann placed very high hopes in the Workers' Movement. Was it the sort of movement that could fulfill his expectations?

The Workers' Movement, which developed during the Second Aliyah, had by the end of the First World War achieved a status which gave it the moral force to demand effort and commitment to the communal interest from the new immigrants who had just arrived — or at least from the young ones. It had a myth, a heroic legend, but it did not have the strength to organize the movement, to unite it and to create a new body in order to tackle the new problem.

The Histadrut was founded by 4,433 young people, who took part in the foundation conference which met in Haifa during Hanukkah 1920. Earlier, at the end of the World War, the Workers' Movement was in fact divided. There were two parties within it, Ahdut Ha'Avodah (the Unity of Labor) on one side and HaPo'el HaTza'ir on the other, and two systems of economic institutions. The two parties and their two institutional systems competed for the body and soul of every new worker and every new immigrant. There was rivalry between leaders, the leaders of the Second Aliyah. An external force was needed which, through its enthusiasm, ambitions and demands, would impose the will to unite on the older and more experienced leadership. The Histadrut was founded, therefore, to a considerable degree, as a result of pressure by the people of the Third Aliyah. The young people who had arrived in the Third Aliyah understood that they were the first to be hurt by the competition between the two parties.

But the Histadrut was not founded only as a trade union. It was founded as an all-inclusive body, which had primarily a national role to fulfill. This was the decisive contribution of the leaders of the Second Aliyah. They saw themselves and their movement as having a national role of the utmost importance even in the days of the Second Aliyah, before the First World War. At the end of the war, before the start of the Third Aliyah, they demanded that the Zionist movement give them full authority to build the country, or, in other words, they asked to serve as a sort of "building contractor" for Zionism. These people did not wish to settle for an organization that would be a mere trade union.

Finally, the Histadrut was founded as a constructive compromise, including within it many different aspects of social action. It included the political parties, which were not disbanded, although some of the Second Aliyah leaders, mainly Berl Katznelson and David Ben Gurion, almost insisted that that should be an essential condition for the foundation of the Histadrut. After prolonged argument, the Histadrut was founded as an organization with three aspects: a union of political parties; a trade union, the function of which was to protect the workers and to improve working conditions; and a constructive institution, which took upon itself to build a new society.

In its practical aspirations and aims, the Histadrut tried to build for the workers a society the members of which would not need any external society. It wished to supply everything and to become a sort of complete socialist autarky. This workers' society was to operate in every field — labor, culture, education, settlement, immigration and Hebrew teaching. The aspirations of the Histadrut, which were largely fulfilled, were, in a way, Utopian; Utopian in the sense of the belief that it was possible to build a perfect society, here and now and not as something that must await the coming of the Messiah. The activism of the public whose leadership founded the Histadrut contributed to this. These Utopian aspirations reached their most extreme form in the idea of the general commune of the workers of Eretz Israel, in the Labor Brigade, named after Joseph Trumpeldor.

This Utopia was not, of course, realized in its entirety. It is doubtful whether it is possible to realize Utopia, but various component parts of it achieved very great success. The national significance of this success was perhaps more important that its social significance, since the Histadrut was active in a number of fields, social and national at the same time. The Histadrut initiated settlement on the land. It was the body behind the workers' settlements of the 'twenties and 'thirties. It build workers' suburbs near the cities, like Shehunat Borochov near Tel Aviv and HaKrayot near Haifa. It build cooperative enterprises in the fields of production and marketing. It provided welfare services, such as the Kupat Holim (sick fund) and other institutions. It built its own educational system, the workers' school network. These social institutions, all touched by a hint of Utopianism, quickly became instruments for achieving national purposes.

The Histadrut also created the national defense organization. We have already indicated that the HaShomer organization arose from the people of the Second Aliyah and, in fact, from the socialists among them. The Histadrut took it under its wing and turned HaShomer into a people's military organization, the Haganah. The Histadrut laid the foundations for national defense, which later, not without struggle, not without arguments or personal tensions, developed into the Israel Defense Forces. It was the Haganah that was available to the Yishuv in the national conflicts in which it was tested in the disturbances of 1921, 1929, 1936 to 1939 and until the outbreak of the War of Independence.

There is no doubt that the crowning achievement of the workers' society or Histadrut society — if one can call it that — that gradually developed, was the communal settlement. The settlement of the Jezreel Valley in the first half of the 1920's became not only the main effort of the Workers' Movement, but also a symbol of its ethos and its myth.

The settlement of the Jezreel Valley was carried out in two ways, which were represented by Ein Harod as a symbol of a collective, communal settlement; and Nahalal, as a symbol of a workers' moshav. A workers' moshav was a kind of combination between collectivism and private enterprise, between commercial public ownership and individual management of private farms.

Three trends operated in the communal movement. The first, the most radical, was realized in the Labor Brigade, which tried to found an inclusive commune of the workers of Eretz Israel. The workers' communal organization ran into opposition on the part of the Histadrut, because, to a certain degree, it claimed to be an alternative to it and had pretensions of putting communal socialist radicalism into practice. It failed because of these pretensions.

The second trend was that of the large, open kibbutz, the symbol of which was Ein Harod. The concept of a "large, open kibbutz" meant a very large collective economic unit, as Shlomo Lavi visualized it. The *large* kibbutz would be a self-sufficient economic unit, capable of supplying all its own needs, economic, cultural and social; it meant a large commune that would be free from the pressures of the capitalist market. The concept of an *"open kibbutz"* meant extreme openness to the needs of society, with intensive involvement in the society outside it, not a band of isolated individuals fleeing from public interests who were wrapped up in their own problems and solved them within their own narrow framework. The kibbutz would be a large body, open in all directions, where people could come and go, and it would be involved in public affairs through its central position in the Workers' Movement and through its envoys' activities in the Zionist movement. It is, therefore, not accidental that the United Kibbutz Movement, which was based on these ideas, has from the beginning of the 'twenties and to the present day been the most active body in the Workers' Movement. In the 1940's, the United Kibbutz Movement took the Palmach under its wing, and it is doubtful whether, without its initiative, the Hebrew defense forces would have had at their disposal the military force that decided the outcome of the struggle before May 1948.

The second model in the communal settlement movement was that of the "kvutzah." This was a small, intimate unit, based on selection intended to produce personal harmony between the members of the group. To a certain extent, there was an inclination toward political segregation in these groups. They had a tendency not to get too involved in political conflicts. Their purpose was, in the words of Zvi Schatz, one of the theorists of the kvutzah movement, to bring redemption to the individual in a disintegrating society. This explains the intimacy, the family atmosphere, the selectivity and the avoidance of political involvement that characterized the kvutzah and differentiated it from the United Kibbutz Movement.

These two types of settlements, the large kibbutz and the kvutzah, were a faithful expression of moods among the young people, who on the one hand were gripped by aspirations for national redemption on a large scale, and on the other yearned, on the personal level, for a fulfilled life in an intimate society.

Beside these, there appeared the HaShomer Hatza'ir kibbutz movement. The HaShomer Hatza'ir kibbutzim mixed the revolutionary enthusiasm of the Labor Brigade with the political involvement of the United Kibbutz Movement and the aesthetic elitism of the kvutzah. The HaShomer Hatza'ir people, who were among the first of the Third Aliyah, were a special phenomenon in the landscape of that aliyah. Most of them came from the Jewish upper middle class, some from a culturally assimilated environment, and brought with them the most advanced progressive phrases and theories which were popular in Europe before and after the war. They were young men and women who sought their personal salvation in labor in this country and saw in national realization a means to individual redemption. Their life experiences in homes of middle class domesticity had been different from those of the other young people, who came from Russia and gathered mainly in the Labor Brigade. The quietness, the introversion, the speculations of the HaShomer Hatza'ir people formed a contrast to the noisiness, the shouting, the joy of life of the Labor Brigade.

The fourth model of workers' settlement was that of the workers' moshav, which tried to combine personal initiative with partial cooperation, particularly in marketing and education.

To tell the truth, there was scarcely a common language between these different movements. Each phenomenon was unique and each made its own contribution. We have mentioned the affair of the Brigade and we must return and stress that its failure left very deep traumatic scars on the soul of the generation. A dispute broke out between the leaders of the Brigade and those of the Histadrut. The dispute was a fundamental one and we shall not inquire here who was right and who was wrong. It concerned the question of the sovereignty of the inclusive body over a part of it and to what extent a part, an active part, could defy the orders of the majority and of the elected leadership in a voluntary society.

A struggle ensued over this question and finally some of the members and most of the leaders of the Labor Brigade left the country, returned to the U.S.S.R., and tried to set up a commune there. This commune failed and the leaders eventually met their deaths in Stalin's persecutions. The failure of the Brigade came as a shock, because it bore witness to the failure of activism. Moreover, there was deep disappointment, arising from the great hopes that had been pinned on the Brigade.

The veteran leaders of the Second Aliyah, who became the leadership of the Histadrut, headed by Ben Gurion, at first saw the Brigade as the shock troops of Zionist realization, like the Palmach of the 1940's. Ben Gurion went further and thought that his party, Ahdut Ha'Avodah, should join the Labor Brigade and become part of it. As the first secretary of the Histadrut, he toyed with the idea of setting up a common fund for all the workers of Eretz Israel — not a commune, but a common fund. There were thus great expectations, for the Brigade was seen as a force that could achieve something. As the members of the Second Aliyah were tired by now and were no longer capable of carrying on front-line, avant-guard activism, while here were these young people who had organized themselves into the Brigade and were prepared to put themselves at the service of the national mission, high hopes were pinned on the Brigade. But, as mentioned, the dispute broke out and the frustration following the disintegration of the Brigade, the arguments and the emigration of the leaders, all left a deep scar on the souls of the leadership and of the entire generation. In addition, there was the controversy between the kvutzot and the kibbutzim, which prevented the foundation of a united movement for the kibbutzim. There was also the fierce dispute between the supporters of the idea of the workers' moshav and those fanatical for the idea of the kibbutz.

Nevertheless, in 1925, at the end of this period, the communal movement numbered twenty six kvutzot and kibbutzim. In addition, there were seventeen different groups preparing for settlement in the villages. There were also seven urban kibbutzim and four women's farms. These last groups were organizations intended to solve the problems of young, single people in the towns, both through communal life for men and women together, and through separate bodies intended only for women workers. Altogether, at this time 2684 members belonged to the communal movement. There were also about five workers' moshavim, which, as mentioned, combined cooperation with private initiative.

Zionism and the Yishuv in Eretz Israel achieved a great deal in the period of the Third Aliyah. First, the political organizational patterns of the Zionist movement and of the Yishuv were created. These were the patterns which led the movement and the Yishuv toward the foundation of the State; We refer here to the Zionist Federation as the representative of the Jewish people, the national institutions of the Yishuv, the Haganah as its military instrument, and the workers' Histadrut as comprising the activist forces that were prepared to put themselves at the disposal of the Zionist movement.

In this period the instruments of settlement were created. All the forms of settlement that later accompanied the Zionist movement and accomplished its tasks, both in the field of mastering the land and of consolidating the boundaries of Jewish settlement — all these instruments, the moshavim, kibbutzim and kvutzot — were created during the Third Aliyah, by the young immigrants of that time.

As a result of organization, of the creation of institutions and of the discovery of the ability to cooperate and to create a common organization in spite of internal differences, a group of leaders appeared on the stage of the Yishuv, who were capable of directing the movement from within, and who later became the leaders of the Yishuv, and later, in the 1930's, the national leadership of the Zionist movement. We are referring to David Ben Gurion, who was the secretary of the Histadrut, Berl Katznelson, Yitzhak Ben Zvi, Yitzhak Tabenkin, Yosef Sprintzak and others. This was the leadership that, through its talents, had already turned the Workers' Movement into the central and determining body in Eretz Israel by the middle of the 1920's. By the end of the 'twenties it was the leading body in the Zionist movement. By the middle of the 'thirties, leading up to the Second World War, it was the leading body of the Jewish people.

IX.

The Period of the Fourth Aliyah

In discussing the Third Aliyah, we stressed the political turning point that occurred with the end of the First World War and the Balfour Declaration. We also stressed the national and political significance of that declaration, which changed the status of the Jewish people in the world and legitimized its settlement in Eretz Israel.

Before we discuss the new period in the history of the Yishuv, that of the Fourth Aliyah, something should be said about the constructive significance of the British government's policy toward the Jewish community in Eretz Israel and to explain its influence on the building program of the Yishuv.

We must return, therefore, to the constructive, creative significance of the Balfour Declaration. Great hopes were raised by the declaration. They were raised by items that were not stated in it in so many words, but were interpreted as favorable to Zionism. The Balfour Declaration fostered the hope that Eretz Israel would be given to the Jews, which meant either a Jewish state in Eretz Israel or Eretz Israel as a Jewish state. The hope was also cherished that the British government would actively assist the building enterprise in Eretz Israel.

But what was written was one thing, while policy was another. The Balfour Declaration read: "His Majesty's Government view with favour the establishment in Palestine of a national home for the Jewish people and will use their best endeavours to facilitate the

75

achievement of this object." It continued by speaking of protecting the rights of the non-Jewish religious communities. With regard to the subject of this book, the national enterprise, it should be emphasized that the British government's commitments were extremely limited and with many reservations. It "views with favour," it "will use its best endeavours to facilitate the achievement of this object." "This object" was the building of the Jewish national home in Eretz Israel.

Despite these limited commitments, there were people who hoped, both immediately after the declaration and in later years, that the British government would do a great deal for the settlement of the Jewish people in Eretz Israel. They expected that a big loan would be given by the government, and through its assistance, by international banking institutions. Some went further and even thought that the British government would help in a huge immigration program. Everyone expected that it would be in the British interest to settle a very large number of Jews in Eretz Israel.

The British leaders, however, thought otherwise. It is true that they hoped, apparently, in their heart of hearts, that a Jewish majority would be created in the country in the next ten years, that is during the 1920's, but they were not prepared to give actual economic aid to such a large scale enterprise. From the beginning, it immediately became clear to them that there were political difficulties, and that the Arab population not only did not accept Zionism, but was actively opposed to it, as was demonstrated in the disturbances. It must also be understood that at the end of the war the British government had economic problems in absorbing the mass of conscripts into industry, and the economic situation did not improve throughout the 1920's.

The government decided that it had to conduct two separate policies in Eretz Israel, one toward the Jews and one toward the Arabs. The Jews were given the opportunity of achieving what they desired by their own efforts, within the bounds of the Mandate, that is within the restrictions of the Balfour Declaration. They were given a sort of autonomy, as regards building the national home without government interference. On the other hand, a paternalistic policy was established toward the Arabs. The officials of the Mandate government saw themselves, to a certain degree, as the guardians of the Arabs, whom them considered both disadvantaged and in need of education.

It should be stressed that the Mandate government achieved a great deal in this country: in the formation of the law, health services, a road system etc. But in many of its acts it consciously gave preference to the Arabs over the Jews, for instance in the awarding of land under government control to Arab farmers, as opposed to the restriction of land grants to Jews. The Arabs were also given preference in employment in the Mandatory civil service, an economic sector that could greatly have eased the unemployment among the Jews.

Nevertheless, through a paradox of history, Jewish autonomy was strengthened precisely because of the fact that the British government, so to speak, relaxed the restrictions on the Jews and enabled them to take action through their own resources, as if to force them to act on their own. The Jews came to understand more and more that what mattered was what the Jews did, rather than what the Gentiles thought about, or intended for them. In this way, the Yishuv was strengthened, through what can perhaps be defined as the craftiness of history.

One of the characteristics of government policy in the field of construction of the Yishuv was the test case of immigration. The existence of the Yishuv depended on immigration; Zionist policy was linked to immigration and the relationship between Zionism and Great Britain was very influenced by this need for immigration.

The Jewish people was not living in its own land. The British government was certainly able to prevent immigration, as it proved by the fact that later, at the end of the 1930's, when it chose to do so, it did prevent it. It was necessary, therefore, to conduct a policy that would enable the continuation of immigration. The importance of the Balfour Declaration is also made clear by this. It is true that it was not the declaration that laid the foundation for the Jewish State — those foundations were laid by Jewish constructive effort — but its effect can also be appreciated by the converse: by what the

British government did not prevent, or rather what it allowed. And it allowed the continuation of immigration, even if in a limited form.

At the beginning of the British occupation of the country, in the years 1917-1919, it continued to be ruled by a military government, which was anti-Zionist and not a little anti-Semitic. The head of this government and its army officers were infected by the anti-Semitism they had acquired from the *Protocols of the Elders of Zion*. Apart from this anti-Semitism derived from books, they were also influenced by the situation in the country. They recognized the balance of power. They saw which was the majority and which the minority. For this reason some of them even recommended not publicizing the Balfour Declaration in Eretz Israel. But the central government in London was opposed to that. At any rate, restrictions were placed on free immigration to Eretz Israel in the days of the military government.

The situation changed with the granting of the Mandate over Eretz Israel by the League of Nations in 1922, when the British government officially accepted the Mandate, and when the first High Commissioner arrived in Eretz Israel. Herbert Samuel was a liberal British statesman of Jewish origin and Zionist tendencies. He was one of the first, at the beginning of the First World War, to propose the idea of creating a Jewish state in Eretz Israel, which would serve as a kind of buffer state between Syria, which was under mainly French influence; and Egypt and above all the Suez Canal, which were under British protection.

On his arrival in the country, Herbert Samuel established an immigration policy that distinguished between two kinds of immigrants. The first category included those with a certain, not large, amount of capital, fixed at 120 pounds sterling, whose immigration to Eretz Israel was virtually unrestricted. They had the right to acquire passports at British consulates in their countries of residence. In the second category were the immigrants who were brought to the country through the agency of the Zionist Federation, which accepted responsibility for them.

Quotas for immigration licenses, known as "certificates," were fixed for the two types. At that time, in 1920, an extremely large quota of certificates was fixed: 16,500, not all of which were used by the Zionist Federation. We have already noted, in the discussion of the Third Aliyah, that at the beginning of the 'twenties the Jewish people made a serious mistake, when it had the chance of mass immigration and did not come. Perhaps this failure to immigrate occurred through the force of inertia, which has great strength in history. The Zionist Federation also, under all its leaders, from Zev Jabotinsky to Chaim Weizmann, hesitated to encourage mass immigration, because of its lack of resources. The fear prevailed that when the masses arrived in the country, there would be nothing there to support them. So the leaders restrained immigration, and the immigration that did occur was largely spontaneous and against the wishes of the Zionist leadership. When the immigrants arrived, they immediately faced economic difficulties, because there was no work for them. Not only had employment opportunities not been planned, but the Zionist Federation did not have the means to create them. In these dark days in the history of the Zionist Federation and of the nation-building enterprise, it was Herbert Samuel, the High Commissioner, who came to the rescue. He introduced a road building programme, and a large number of the Third Aliyah immigrants found work paving roads. The roads from Haifa to Nazareth, from Tiberias to Migdal, and others absorbed many of the young people of the Third Aliyah and were also the scene of a particular way of life at that time.

The Mandate government headed by Herbert Samuel, whether with Zionist intent or not, thus assisted the constructive enterprise. The situation changed with the outbreak of the disturbances in May 1921. These disturbances claimed many Jewish lives, among them the writer Joseph Chaim Brenner, and caused the British government to have second thoughts about the policy of almost unlimited immigration that had prevailed between 1920 and the disturbances of 1921.

The first reaction of the High Commissioner to the disturbances was the suspension of immigration, and that was a sign of what was to follow, immigration becoming a means of political pressure.

Later, when the storm had died down, a new immigration policy was determined, in the official "White Paper" known by the name of the Colonial Secretary of that time, Winston Churchill, and published in 1922. This document was, in fact, written by Herbert Samuel, but was referred to as Churchill's because he was the Colonial Secretary. Churchill, incidentally, favored Zionism, and, when one examines his entire career, it is clear that, in fact, he continued to favor it, within the guidelines of the White Paper of 1922.

This document, for the first time, commented publicly on the Balfour Declaration, and certain things were stated clearly and definitely. The principles on which it was based affected the Jews primarily. Jews had the right to immigrate to and settle in Eretz Israel, and to build their national home in Eretz Israel, but they did not have a right to the whole of the country. In fact, the White Paper established the principle of the first partition of Eretz Israel, in that a distinction was made between eastern and western Eretz Israel. Eastern Eretz Israel was awarded to a member of the Hashemite family, Prince Abdullah. What is more important for our purpose, it was determined that future immigration to Eretz Israel should be in accordance with the economic capacity of the land to absorb it.

The concept of "absorptive capacity of the land" could be interpreted in two ways. The first interpretation was the absorptive capacity of the entire economy, that is the Jewish and Arab sectors together. The second interpretation was the absorptive capacity of the Jewish sector alone. The second interpretation was more convenient for the Jews, since in that case unemployment among the Arabs would not affect the calculations of immigration officials, or those appointed to fix immigration quotas. In practice, in calculations of the economic situation, only the demand for workers in the Jewish sector was taken into account, not the situation in the Arab sector.

It was determined once again that the immigrants were to be divided into two categories, those who were independent, and those who depended on the Zionist Federation. For the independent ones, the property qualification was raised from 120 to 500 pounds sterling. It was also decided that members of the free professions should be included in this category, along with relatives in the first degree, such as brothers, sisters and parents; people in demand by employers; and men of religion. These had the right to apply to embassies for immigration permits.

The second category was of immigrant workers dependent on the Zionist Federation. Its immigration quota was fixed every year through negotiation between the government and the Jewish Agency. These negotiations were very important to the Zionist movement, but were also very important in the eyes of the officials. In their course the Agency representatives were always raising and increasing the numbers demanded, while the government officials reduced them. On average, throughout the 1920's, the Agency received about one third of what it demanded from year to year. Afterwards, of course, there were complaints, but that was the situation.

The Fourth Aliyah reached Eretz Israel within the terms of the arrangement established in the White Paper of 1922. The Fourth Aliyah, as will be seen below, was the first mass aliyah, and as such is proof that under certain circumstances mass aliyah was possible, even within the restrictions imposed by the Mandate government. So, when we discuss the insufficient achievements of the Zionist enterprise, we should not put the blame entirely on others, but should also scrutinize our own actions.

The Third Aliyah ended in a crisis. But in 1924 the immigrants who opened the Fourth Aliyah phase began to arrive on the shores of Eretz Israel. Why did the Fourth Aliyah take place? Why was it a mass immigration? There were two reasons. The first was anti-Semitic pressure in Poland, with the policy of economic discrimination associated with the name of Grabski, who was Interior Minister in Poland. That gave this aliyah its nickname, Grabski's Aliyah.

But anti-Semitic pressure on its own never brings people to Eretz Israel. We have already seen that in earlier periods, whenever the situation of the Jews deteriorated, the vast majority of them migrated to the U.S.A. Here something else happened, more significant and perhaps even fateful in the history of Israel. Between

1922 and 1924 very severe restrictions were imposed on entry into the United States. Under pressure from public opinion, the United States government decided to limit immigration into the country for fear of altering the composition of its population. Among others, the Jews suffered from this. In 1924 the gates of mass immigration were, in effect, slammed in the Jews' faces and they had nowhere to go. Naturally, Eretz Israel became an alternative to the U.S.A. for this mass migration. Thus the masses came to try out Eretz Israel as a solution to their distressed situation.

We have said that the restrictions on migration were fateful, for it is very likely that this was the beginning of the Jewish Holocaust. When Fascism arose, European Jewry faced extermination, and had nowhere to turn. These restrictions were also proof of the justice of Zionism's claims, raised in the name of pioneering idealism and mass distress. Here, for the first time, the distress of the masses of the Jewish people was being demonstrated. No distress can be greater than the tragic trap into which the Jews of Europe fell between the publication of the restrictions on immigration into the United States and the end of the Second World War. Part of this period was marked by mass immigration to the State of Israel and it showed that the answer to the suffering of the Jewish masses lay only in the Jewish State.

X.

Between Achievement and Failure

The Fourth Aliyah was the first mass aliyah in the history of the renewed Jewish settlement of Eretz Israel. In the years 1924 to 1930 about 80,000 immigrants arrived in the country. In one year, 1925, 34,000 people came. For the Yishuv, which numbered 100,000 people at that time, this meant an addition of about one third in a single year, an enormous proportion for any society absorbing immigration. Even if we subtract from the number of immigrants that of the emigrants, of whom there were many in the second half of the 'twenties, the net gain was about 60,000. As a result, the Jewish population of Eretz Israel grew from 100,000 in the middle of the 'twenties to about 180,000 at the end of the decade.

Most of the immigrants were from the middle class, those who had proved that they owned property worth 500 pounds sterling. This aliyah was accompanied by a flow of private capital, something unknown in its scope in earlier periods. Twelve million pounds sterling were invested in land at this time. Most of the economic development was, of course, in the cities, particularly Tel Aviv. It was the Fourth Aliyah that brought about the flowering of the first Hebrew city.

In the cities, the building industry prospered, of course, this being the leading economic sector. Following on this accelerated building, the price of urban land rose. As a result wages and the cost of living also rose, as did speculation in building plots, land, etc. This growth was not restricted only to building. It also reached the industrial sector. The Lodzia factory, which laid the foundations of the textile industry in the country, was founded at this time, as was the Shemen factory. Nor did this growth pass over agriculture. Between 1925 and 1930 the citrus sector, which was in Jewish hands, grew six-fold.

New settlements, such as Herzliya, Magdiel and Raanana, were also founded. A particular innovation at that time was the participation of organized religious Jewry in the Zionist movement and of part of it even in the settlement enterprise. This led to the foundation of Kfar Hasidim and Sde Ya'acov on the banks of the River Kishon and in the Jezreel Valley. At the end of the period two enterprises were founded, which were to be of the greatest importance for the industrial future of the country. The first was the potash operation in Sodom, established through the initiative of Novomyaiski. The second was the power station at Naharayim, which was the pet project of the great initiator and Zionist leader, Pinchas Rutenberg. These two projects were the foundation stone of industry and exports by the Jews of Eretz Israel.

The whole period from 1924 to 1930 can be divided into three subordinate periods. The first, that of the economic boom, lasted only two years, from early 1924 until the end of 1925. After it came the economic slump and social despair that lasted from 1926 to the end of 1927 or the beginning of 1928. The third period was that of recovery. It lasted from late 1928 to late 1930.

In the boom period a quantitative change occurred in the history of the Yishuv. The quantitative expansion in the economy and the demographic growth brought about a qualitative change. The social composition of the Yishuv began to change. For the first time since the Balfour Declaration there appeared a new social force, which took upon itself the task of the economic building of the Yishuv. This was the bourgeoisie. The Fourth Aliyah, if one may use such terms, restored to the bourgeoisie their self-respect in Zionist terms. More and more people became convinced that from this time onwards the process of "normal" settlement was beginning in Eretz Israel, that is settlement by property-owners, and that it was they who would build the country. There were also those who went further and claimed that the pioneering role of the middle class was now beginning.

This development also had political implications, which we shall examine presently. The first appearance of the Revisionist movement in the middle of the 1920's and its rising strength were associated with the same bourgeois hope. Zev Jabotinsky saw himself as the leader of the new wave of Zionist construction. On the other hand, the Workers' Movement, which had carried on its shoulders the burden of the building of Eretz Israel throughout the Third Aliyah period, viewed the new wave of the Fourth Aliyah with mixed feelings. It was pleased to see the phenomenon of mass aliyah. After all, from the beginning the Workers' Movement had looked forward to the masses of Jews who would come to Eretz Israel. But it was also apprehensive of this aliyah.

It was apprehensive for two reasons, first because here suddenly was a new social alternative, which was likely, as seemed logical, to push the Workers' Movement from the center of Zionist activity, with all that was implicit in this for that movement.

The second reason was that the Workers' Movement viewed with suspicion the social and economic trends of this aliyah. The movement claimed that this aliyah invested the best part of its capital in non-productive fields, building, of course, being non-productive. The rise in land prices and the speculation in building plots that occurred at that time all aroused the fears of the Workers' Movement that the Diaspora, from which they had wished to escape, was arriving and renewing itself here in Eretz Israel.

These suspicions were also shared by some members of the Zionist leadership. Chaim Weizmann was no less suspicious of this aliyah than the Workers' Movement was. He expressed this suspicion, extremely strongly, when he said in the Zionist Congress of 1924 that he did not wish to build a "second Nalewski" in Eretz Israel. Nalewski was a famous street in the Jewish quarter of Warsaw and the Zionists saw it as one of the symbols of the Diaspora. For this he was showered with abuse and contempt by those who saw themselves as builders of the country. They responded to the Workers' Movement and to Weizmann by calling the settlement enterprise of the Workers' Movement "eaters of the bread of charity," fed from the Zionist movement's table, contributing nothing and merely wasting money.

In any case, the growth was great and the expectations of change were also great. Then, at the end of 1925, the signs of crisis for this aliyah began to be apparent. This crisis had a number of different causes, some internal and other external. The external ones were connected with changes in financial policy, both in the country from which this aliyah originated, Poland, and in the currency fluctuations of the British government. In Poland there was a devaluation of the local currency, the zloty, and the British government revalued the pound sterling. The result was that the capital which the immigrants brought with them declined in value. From now on they received fewer pounds sterling in exchange for their zlotys, and, with this reduction in their capital, an economic crisis broke out. Investment was limited, it was difficult to pay debts, to continue to buy land, to pay high wages. The result was immediate unemployment.

Unemployment, of course, led to emigration. The decline in immigration was very steep. In 1927 the migration balance was negative. In contrast to 3,000 immigrants, 5,000 people left the country. This crisis was a tragedy for the middle class, of many good and innocent people who invested most of their money in Eretz Israel and within a very short period of time found themselves facing bankruptcy, with virtually no one to help them, as they lost all their property and were down to their last crust of bread. Public concerns went bankrupt as well. One of the most important enterprises of the Workers' Movement, Solel Boneh, went bankrupt, and that was a tragedy for the Workers' Movement. In those years there was a question mark hanging over the whole movement. People became more and more doubtful of the future of the entire Zionist enterprise, all the more since the economic situation in Europe was then beginning to improve. The gap between the improving economic situation in Europe and the recession in Eretz Israel brought Zionist morale to rock bottom.

One of the signs of this recession was seen in the behavior of

Jewish bodies in the United States — the non-Zionist, philanthropic organizations, that were prepared to aid Jews. Instead of investing money in Eretz Israel, they gave assistance, to the amount of millions of dollars, to the Jewish settlement project in the Crimea, in Communist Russia. On the other hand, and in a paradoxical way, the recession and the crisis of the Fourth Aliyah actually strengthened the self-confidence of the Workers' Movement. It became clear to its leaders, and to the Zionist leadership that was close to them in outlook, that there was no middle class alternative of purely private initiative to the Zionist construction enterprise. It was, in fact, necessary to return to the earlier method, to the method of public initiative in raising national capital, and of the Workers' Movement as the practical arm of the enterprise, the one which would do the work. It was not coincidental that at the end of the period the political pact between Chaim Weizmann and the Workers' Movement of Eretz Israel was strengthened. With the foundation of Mapai (The Party of the Workers of Eretz Israel) in 1930, it became the leading force in Zionism.

By 1928, the recovery was already perceptible. It arose from the growing weight of imported public capital, mainly from Zionist movement funds. The movement committed itself to solving the crisis, and in this it had a partial success. The role of Chaim Weizmann at this time and in this field was decisive. He was the one who went out to Jewish communities, particularly those of the United States, and pleaded with them to contribute funds to save the enterprise in Eretz Israel. In addition, there began the building of the economic public concerns already mentioned, like the potash industry in Sodom and the power station at Naharayim. These projects offered employment to the workers, and the very fact of their establishment and operation greatly improved public morale in the country.

Towards the end of the period, in 1929, the Jewish Agency was founded. It must be understood that it was founded as a body in which the Zionist movement and non-Zionist Jewish organizations would cooperate. The foundation of the Jewish Agency on the basis of cooperation between Zionists and non-Zionists in one organization was, in a way, the first sign that the Jewish people in its entirety was ready to be co-opted, mainly through its capital, on behalf of the building of Eretz Israel.

Many hopes were placed in the Jewish Agency and this also helped to raise morale. These hopes were not fulfilled, but at the time they marked a turning point. Even those opposed to the foundation of the Agency, those who saw this institution as an undemocratic organization because its non-Zionist representatives were not elected by the people, were prepared to support this organization. The outstanding example was the decision of the Workers' Movement, after many doubts, to support Weizmann in this process, because of the hope of attracting resources for the building of Eretz Israel.

But immediately after the establishment of the Jewish Agency, in the very same year, came the death of Louis Marshall, the chairman of the American Jewish Council, who, together with Weizmann, had initiated the setting up of the Agency. His death removed the one person who was most able to attract American capitalists to the project. In addition, disturbances broke out in Eretz Israel, on a wider scale than before, offering clear evidence of the birth of a nationalist Arab movement opposed to Zionism. These disturbances greatly shocked the Jews. But this shock, paradoxically, did not harm the building enterprise. As a result of these incidents, the tragedy that had struck the Jews of Eretz Israel and the cruelty of the disturbances, much wider circles were persuaded to support Zionism, though at that stage this had no financial significance. The turning point in this area came two to three years later, with the beginning of the Fifth Aliyah, which began to stream toward Eretz Israel in different circumstances from those of the 'twenties.

To sum up this chapter in the history of Zionist construction, it can be said that the decade of the 1920's was perhaps the decisive decade in establishing the nature of the Zionist enterprise in Eretz Israel, that is establishing the character of the Jewish society of the country. The institutional system of Jewish autonomy was built in this decade. In the 1920's the Yishuv of Eretz Israel became the body responsible above all others for its own fate. Awareness grew that the fate of the enterprise rested primarily with the Jews and not with the British government. This awareness greatly helped the enterprise itself.

In this decade, a clear distinction was established between the urban and rural economies. This period determined the urban character of the Jewish community of Eretz Israel. Commerce, crafts and industry all developed. Types of communal settlement were crystallized. It was not only that the movement of kibbutzim and kvutzot spread, but that national organizations of communal settlements were founded.

In 1927 HaKibbutz HaMeuchad (the United Kibbutz Movement) was founded as a national organization, as was HaKibbutz Ha'Artzi (the National Kibbutz Movement) of the HaShomer HaTza'ir movement, and, at the end of the period, in the early 1930's, the Moshav movement as well. Because of their centralization and their national character, these bodies greatly assisted the continuation of settlement in the 1930's, the period in which settlement became, in a way, an instrument for realizing the national and security policy of the Zionist movement.

The constructivist trend in the Zionist movement itself was greatly strengthened in this period. The Zionist institutions invested more and more money into building and, as we have already seen, the national funds managed by the Zionist movement became the decisive factor and the vital means in overcoming the economic recession of the crisis period.

Political molds were also being set at this time. The dispute in the Zionist Federation between Weizmann and Brandeis resulted in a decisive victory for Weizmann. From now on the Zionist Federation represented the whole range of problems affecting the Jewish people and the whole range of the problems of the Zionist enterprise in Eretz Israel. The coalition — the pact between Weizmann and the Workers' Movement — became more and more actual in the course of the 1920's and achieved active realization in 1930, at the end of the period. The Revisionist opposition had appeared in the Zionist Federation and had become an active anti-establishment factor outside it as well, when Zev Jabotinsky attempted to found an alternative Zionist federation.

In all these ways, the 1920's were *the* formative period, the period that determined the character and the appearance of the Yishuv in Eretz Israel.

XI.

The Period of the Fifth Aliyah

The Fourth Aliyah came to an end, in effect, at the end of the 1920's. The period that followed, in the 1930's — the period of the Fifth Aliyah — was very different from the one that preceded it. We have already indicated that the crisis period in the history of the Jewish people began as far back as the 1870's and continued almost until the present day. The anti-Semitic movement in Europe, the anti-Jewish policies of governments, the First World War, and the Bolshevik revolution in Russia, all directly or indirectly put heavy pressure on the Jewish people, and eventually led even to a change in the course of its history.

Until the beginning of the 1930's, these pressures did not yet question the existence of the Jewish people. But by the early 1930's the situation had changed, with the rise of Fascism in Europe and the growth of anti-Semitism in the countries of Eastern Europe. We shall try to examine the connection between political events, external and internal developments affecting Eretz Israel, and the building enterprise. We shall see how, paradoxically, this emergency period was actually one of expansion in the building program and we will try to explain it.

First, let us discuss the political developments. The general political background was marked by the rise to power of Fascism in Europe, Nazism in Germany and anti-Semitism in Eastern Europe. As mentioned, these threatened the existence of the Jewish people, even if in the 1930's the awareness of the Holocaust had not yet penetrated the consciousness of the Jewish people, in particular that of its leaders. But the Jewish people was under pressure, and that pressure affected migration. There was a growing tendency to leave, to flee from the trouble centers, but the gates of salvation were closed.

As a result of the restrictions on immigration imposed by the United States in the middle of the 1920's, that country ceased to be a solution to the problem of mass Jewish distress. At the same time, or later, no other country was prepared to take upon itself the responsibility of dealing with the problem of the Jewish masses. The problem was not only that of the Jews of Germany, persecuted by the Nazi regime, but also of the millions of Jews of Poland and of Hungary as well. The western democracies were afraid to open their borders to a flood of Jewish refugees, for both economic and cultural reasons.

At the same time, Eretz Israel became the main destination of Jewish migration. In the 1930's more Jews, in absolute numbers, immigrated to Eretz Israel than to the United States. Eretz Israel took in one third of all Jewish migrants and, were it not for the limitations which had been imposed on Jewish immigration to Eretz Israel in the second half of the 1930's, the country would undoubtedly have absorbed the vast majority of Jewish refugees who were still able to escape before the outbreak of the Second World War.

But the development was to the detriment of the Jewish people within Eretz Israel as well as outside its borders. In Eretz Israel, following the interference of the Fascist powers of Germany and Italy in the region, and the growth in Jewish immigration in the middle of the 1930's, an Arab revolt broke out in 1934 and 1935 against the Mandate government and against the Jewish community in the country. This revolt bore all the signs of a national uprising in organization, in its ability to impose a reasonable degree of national discipline, in fighting ability, and in the readiness of its people to sacrifice themselves. Alongside these, there were, of course, incidents of robbery and murder, the work of the "gangs."

The Arab revolt lasted for three years, from 1936 to 1939. It

92

severely affected the activities of the Zionist movement and of the construction program. These disturbances did not pass without influencing the Zionist movement itself. As a result of the disturbances, a Royal Commission of Inquiry, the Peel Commission, arrived in the country, dispatched by the British government. In 1937 it made a revolutionary pronouncement: there were two nations in Eretz Israel and there was no possibility of these nations growing closer to each other and living together, because there existed a general societal gap between them at the time, and that gap would widen in the future. The Commission's revolutionary conclusion was, therefore, to partition Eretz Israel into two states, a small Jewish state and a much larger Arab state. Part of Eretz Israel would be kept under British protection — mainly Jerusalem and the southern Negev. The area, which, according to the Commission's recommendations, was to be granted to the Jews, comprised, roughly, a quarter of western Eretz Israel.

This was a revolutionary recommendation, because it meant the end of the Mandate. To begin with, the British government gave the idea a favorable reception, but very quickly, in 1938, it dropped it. There were two reasons for this: the wish to appease the Arabs and the preparations for world war. Once it had penetrated the awareness of the British leadership that there was no avoiding an armed conflict with Germany, it was forced to secure its rear, and the routes of the Middle East, linking the Suez Canal and India, and the oil wells of the region, were very important to it.

For these reasons, Great Britain withdrew from the partition plan and attempted to find another way. This was expressed in the White Paper of 1939, which was also revolutionary in its principles, as opposed to the Balfour Declaration and the Mandate. It also meant the end of the Mandate, but instead of establishing two states it would set up one democratic Palestinian state. This meant a state of the inhabitants of Eretz Israel, in which, of course, the Arab majority would rule, through its democratic weight, and the Jewish minority would be guaranteed certain rights.

In practice, what was intended was the setting up of some sort of cultural Jewish autonomy in Eretz Israel, which meant the end of the Zionist dream, the end of the Balfour Declaration, and the establishment of a Palestinian state. Of course, Zionist policy of the time was forced to respond to the two plans that came one after the other, first to the partition plan and, later, on the eve of the Second World War, to the White Paper plan of 1939. There were very serious differences of opinion within the Zionist movement and it seemed at times as if the movement came close to splitting.

The division between those who accepted and those who rejected the partition plan did not follow party lines. Mapai, the largest party, that led the Zionist Federation along with Chaim Weizmann, was split between those who accepted the plan, led by Ben Gurion, and those who rejected it, led by Berl Katznelson and Tabenkin, who were utterly opposed.

The final confrontation between the two camps was prevented by the change in the Mandate government policy and by the appearance of the White Paper. The Zionist movement had to react to this policy, which was, in its eyes, one of betrayal.

The question which must be asked concerning the Jewish people as a whole in the 1930's and the years of the Second World War, is whether the Jews did all they could to save some of their people from extermination. Did the Zionist movement do enough in its political struggles to establish a state? It is reasonable to assume that if a Jewish state had been set up in Eretz Israel in the 1930's, it would have been possible to save hundreds of thousands, or even a million or more Jews from the extermination camps. I am not maintaining that this struggle was practical at the time. But would a change in the traditional policy of the Zionist movement, going as far as open conflict with the British government, have led to the establishment of a Jewish state before the outbreak of the Second World War?

The second question in whether the Jewish people and the Yishuv did enough to save Jews, to arouse world public opinion, once it was known that they were being exterminated in the camps.

It is true that these hard questions touch on Zionist construction, but the answers lie outside the scope of our discussion. We shall deal with the question of whether the Zionist movement did the maximum in Eretz Israel to continue the building of the economic, demographic and cultural basis, on which arose the Jewish state. It appears that, in contrast to possible failures or abstentions from action in various other fields, in was precisely in this area that the movement performed a revolutionary act, one which laid the foundations for what was to come later.

This revolutionary act was performed in the field of construction, the traditional field of Zionist activity. The greatest efforts of the Zionist movement had always been directed toward that goal, and in this it was a continuation of the enterprise that had begun in the days of the Second Aliyah.

Both spontaneous and directed forces operated together in the Fifth Aliyah, which, as mentioned, began in 1931 and continued until 1939. The spontaneous forces were seen in the large scale, almost mass exodus of Jews from Europe, Jews escaping from the threat of the Nazi regime in Germany and from anti-Semitism in Poland. The greater part of them came to Eretz Israel. The Fifth Aliyah was, in effect, the second episode of mass aliyah, which we have already seen in the 1920's.

More than a quarter of a million immigrants arrived in the country at that time. The whole period can be divided into two subordinate periods. The first, from 1931 to 1936, was the boom period and the second, from 1936 to 1939, was the slump. In the boom, 160,000 people came to the country legally and there were also immigrants who came in unofficial ways. In one year, 1935, there were 65,000 immigrants. In 1934, a year earlier, there were 42,000. It should be remembered that 34,000 came in 1925. Those years, from the mid-twenties to the mid-thirties, were years of mass aliyah in all senses, economic, social and cultural. The inflow of building capital was also unparalleled. At that time, between 1931 and 1936, the capital inflow to the country reached 35 million pounds sterling. In comparison, throughout the 'twenties decade, from 1921 to 1931, the sum of 20 million pounds sterling was brought to the country. The effect was large and very significant.

Three quarters of the immigrants were absorbed in the cities. The urbanizing trend, which commenced at the beginning of the

1920's, therefore gathered greater strength and impetus. As in the 'twenties, construction was the leading sector in economic development in the 'thirties as well, and after it followed manufacturing, industry and agriculture.

It should be remembered and stressed that a great and significant change occurred in the social composition of aliyah. In the 1920's the immigrants came mainly from Eastern Europe, principally Poland. This was also the case with the Fourth Aliyah, though there was more variety in this period and there also appeared immigrants from Western Europe, particularly Germany. The German immigrants were not the majority; they comprised only 20%, but they brought with them the concepts and the standards of the western world, and they made a contribution to the fields of culture, industry, commerce and banking. They were not easily absorbed socially. On the contrary, their social absorption was an agonizing process. The East Europeans did not accept them easily; to some extent they even despised them. They were a different, sometimes even strange, branch of the Jewish people, as seen against the general background, which was mainly East European.

The second period was that of the slump. The decline came, as in the Fourth Aliyah, but not for the same reasons. This was part of the same fateful cycle that pursued the other waves of aliyah, particularly those of mass aliyah. It began with expansion and great expectations, and ended in crisis. As in the Fourth Aliyah, there were both external and internal reasons for that crisis. The external cause was the invasion of Abyssinia by Italy in the mid-thirties, which upset the entire international situation and led to the withdrawal of bank deposits. As a result there was a reduction in the capital intended for financing the economic sector.

The internal cause of the crisis, as in the Fourth Aliyah, arose from unbalanced investment. Most of the capital was invested in the service sector, among them residential building and trade. On the other hand, only a small amount was invested in the productive sectors, such as industry and agriculture. And, as in the Fourth Aliyah, the construction sector was the first to suffer. As this sector had led in the economic expansion, it now led in recession.

The crisis was accompanied, of course, by the phenomenon of unemployment, but this time there was no emigration. Why was there no emigration? Because there was nowhere to which to emigrate. From this point of view, in a tragic fashion, as it were, the prognosis of Zionism was beginning to be realized; that is Jews were being pushed out of non-Jewish society and had nowhere to go.

At the same time it must be stressed that, despite the crisis, the contribution of the Fifth Aliyah was very great. The Jewish population grew to more than 450,000. This meant, from the national point of view, that the earlier Jewish population of 180,000, the existence of which had been put in doubt by both national and economic factors - the Arab opposition and the crisis which affected it — now became a self-supporting national entity. This was the reason why the Peel Commission maintained that there was a Jewish national entity in Eretz Israel and that it was necessary to solve its problem by treating it as a national entity. From this point of view, 1937 was a precedent for 1947. At this time, the precedent was created of the idea of partitioning Eretz Israel between the two peoples, as the single political solution that was both possible and realistic.

The quantitative change that occurred at this time also affected the Jewish-Arab conflict. It should be remembered, and we shall return to this point, that the years 1936-1939 were a testing time for the Yishuv. The struggle between the Jews and the British on the one hand, and the Jews and the Arabs on the other, continued during those three years. The Jews had to hold their own in that struggle and to find new ways of doing so. The fact that they could hold their own was also a function of numbers. A small Yishuv could not have carried on a three year long conflict. From this point of view also, the achievement of the Fifth Aliyah was immense.

Up to now we have been discussing a development which can be defined as automatic, one event leading to another. The Zionist Federation did not initiate the forces operating on the Jews of Europe. They came on their own initiative. All that the Zionist Federation could offer was a solution, and a partial solution at that. But the aliyah came on its own initiative, under force of circumstances. That was also the case regarding the inflow of capital, which was mainly private and invested in Eretz Israel for lack of alternatives. But in the national trial of the second phase, the time of recession, it was the directing forces of the national institutions of the organized movements: of the settlement movement and of the security organization, which made possible the continued existence of the Yishuv under conditions of pressure, and gave it the means to break through the siege imposed on it. These established the precedents, both in settlement and in defense, that ensured the Yishuv and the possibility of embarking on a second battle, about ten years later, in 1947, for the establishment of the State.

XII.

Settlement at the Time of the National Struggle

At the end of the last chapter, in which we discussed the importance and the achievements of the Fifth Aliyah in general, it was stressed that in the crisis period, the national effort determined the fate of the Yishuv. The crowning achievement of the national effort at that time was in settlement. In the 1930's we can distinguish many different trends in settlement. There was the settlement of the German immigrants, as at Nehariya, Kfar Shemaryahu etc. That was enough to prove that the contribution of these immigrants was not limited merely to the urban sector, but was also expressed in settlement. There was an attempt to settle about one thousand workers' families in villages, in workers' moshavim, or in other forms of settlement. While the actual number was far lower than that, this project, which took place mainly in the Sharon, was called the "Settlement of the Thousand." There was also settlement in the Hefer Valley, as at Kfar Vitkin.

The greatest effort was invested in the years from 1936 to 1939, in the "Tower and Stockade" settlement. What was remarkable of this form of settlement was principally its comprehensiveness and the number of settlements that arose on the ground in those three years — which reached a total of 55. In the history of immigration to Eretz Israel, settlement on the land had never until then reached such a heightened pitch.

Another remarkable fact of these settlements was their security function, which had been planned in advance. This course of settlement was intended to put Zionist strategy into action. This strategy, established immediately after the outbreak of the disturbances and in force until the foundation of the State and even after that, was designed to ensure two things: the best possible partition borders for a future state, and the security of the existing Jewish area. From the time when the possibility of partitioning Eretz Israel into two states arose in 1937, the Zionist Federation sought to ensure the best possible borders for the future state, if it should arise. It did not have a better instrument for achieving this goal than cooperative settlements.

At a later stage, after the withdrawal of the partition plan, this settlement was a way of staking a Jewish claim to places where they had not settled earlier. For both reasons, settlement became the political arm of the Zionist movement. Creating facts through settlement became an established principle of Zionist policy.

"Tower and Stockade Settlement" was what the name implied. It was an innovative form of settlement, for these people settled in remote, dangerous places, sometimes cut off from the nearby Jewish settlements, sometimes in the heart of an Arab region. They sought and found appropriate methods for surviving in isolated and dangerous conditions. Prefabricated sections of the new settlement's tower and stockade were brought to the site at dawn. During the day, from early morning to nightfall, the stockade was erected from wood panels, between which were poured gravel and concrete. In the center of the enclosure the tower was erected, on which was installed a searchlight operated by a generator. The tents, or huts, stood within the stockade, with a wire fence strung around them. In this way, a fortified settlement was established within a matter of hours. It was something of a surprise, both to the British authorities and to the Arabs, who conspired against settlement.

The settlements, as mentioned were spread along the borders. At this stage, in the 1930's, they were spread along the northern and northeastern borders: Dan, Dafna, and Sha'ar HaGolan in the north; Massada and Ein Gev in the northeast; Hanita and others along the northwest border. Because of the fear that the partition plan would bar wide areas from Jewish settlement, a breakthrough was made into areas where there had been no previous Jewish settlement, as, for example, Tel Amal in the Beit She'an Valley, which was the first "Tower and Stockade" settlement, and Maoz Haim and Tirat Zvi, of the religious kibbutz movement. Attempts were also made to create continuous strips of settlements to protect communication routes, like Kibbutz Ein HaShofet in the Ephraim Hills and Maale HaHamisha on the road to Jerusalem.

All sections of the Yishuv participated in founding these settlements; immigrants from many countries: Germany, Bulgaria, Poland and the United States; the Eretz Israel youth movements; and the training groups that came from abroad. All the settlement movements took part in this enterprise, from HaShomer HaTza'ir, the United Kibbutz Movement, the Kvutzot Association and the moshavim, to the Religious Kibbutz Movement and the Revisionist movement, Betar. They all participated in this immense effort, to some extent or another. The fact of general settlement served, however, as evidence for the correctness of the idea of constructivism as a method of realizing national ends.

It was this enterprise that, in effect, established the borders of the Jewish State. We shall return to that point. With the outbreak of the Second World War, the same trends continued in the development of the Jewish economy of Eretz Israel and in settlement as before the war. Here we must note the difference between the situation of the Yishuv in Eretz Israel in the First World War and that in the Second World War. While development was frozen during the First World War and the Yishuv even shrank for various reasons, during the Second World War development continued and there was even a certain growth, not actually demographic growth, but growth in the economic area.

This growth should be attributed mainly to the presence of the British army in Eretz Israel and in the region. This army was a large consumer of the products of the Jewish economy. So, there was, for example, a sudden expansion of industry during the war. In the years 1937 to 1943 the number of industrial enterprises doubled, while output increased five times. There were also great developments in agriculture, because Jewish agriculture became the principal supplier of agricultural produce to the Jewish urban market and, to a great extent, to the British army as well.

The standard of living of the Yishuv rose. Here is one of the greatest and saddest paradoxes of history; while the Jewish people in Europe were tortured and destroyed, the situation of the Yishuv improved during the war, both economically and in other ways.

During the war and immediately after it, from 1940 to 1947, settlement continued at a rate not much slower than that of the second half of the 1930's, the period of the "Tower and Stockade." In those seven years, eighty four settlements were established. But while in the "Tower and Stockade" period the emphasis had been placed on the northern, northeastern and eastern borders, during the war and the later 1940's, the emphasis was on the south.

In 1943 the first settlements were set up in the Negev. These were Gvulot, Revivim, Beit Eshel and Beerot Yitzhak. At first they were established as observation points, intended to examine the conditions and the possibilities of further settlement. But in 1946, following the experience of these observation points and under stress of the national needs that arose at that time, eleven settlements were set up in the Negev at the same time. The Kfar Etzion settlements on the way to Hebron should also be mentioned. They were created through the cooperation of two settlement movements, the religious movement and HaShomer HaTza'ir. It was these settlements that established a political fact and it is largely thanks to them that the Negev was attached to the Jewish state by the decision of the commission that partitioned Eretz Israel.

Thus, as mentioned, the trend that became apparent in the second half of the 1930's continued in the 1940's; settlement became a national instrument, the one that accompanied national ends.

To sum up the period that stretched from 1931 to the eve of the establishment of the State, it can be said that in the 1930's and 1940's the numerical basis was laid down for the foundation of the State of Israel; numerical, firstly, in the demographic sense. In 1930 there were 180,000 Jews in Eretz Israel. In 1939 there were 450,000 and in 1947 more than 600,000, nearly 650,000. Thus the Jewish national entity was created.

We have stressed the "numerical basis" in order to differentiate it from earlier periods, in which the qualitative basis was established, for in this emergency period no social innovations were created, no new institutions were established. Everything that had been founded earlier, up to and including the Fourth Aliyah period, developed, grew and expanded numerically in the 'thirties and the first half of the 'forties.

From this we can see the special connection in Zionism between quantity and quality, or rather, in historical order, between quality and quantity, since one completes the other and cannot exist without it.

The quantitative dimension was also expressed in the growth of a modern economy in both agriculture and industry. In particular, one should stress the fast development during the war years and the indirect assistance which the British army gave to this economy, without intending to do so.

We have also mentioned, and shall repeat here, that these were the years of military testing. The disturbances, or the Arab Revolt of 1936 to 1939, the Jewish reaction to that revolt, the ability to withstand it, the ability to apply new methods of fighting, and, later, the conscription to the British army on one hand, and the creation of the Haganah strike force, the Palmach on the other — a force which was associated, both in a social and economic sense, and spiritually with the cooperative settlement movement — all these were expressions of the numerical dimensions of this period.

What is apparent in this period is the decisive weight, in the national sense, of public initiative. Here we must mention the historic controversy that began at the time of the Second Aliyah, as to what was the decisive factor in the building of the Yishuv, private capital and personal initiative, or national capital and public initiative? There were differences of opinion on this point, and not only in the sense of class disagreements — with the Workers' Movement in favor of national capital, while the bourgeoisie favored private capital. In the Workers' Movement there were also orthodox socialists who believed that the country would be build by capitalist finance and private initiative, and that the workers would play only a minor role. On the other hand, the majority believed that the land would be rebuild through national capital, by public initiative and by the Workers' Movement.

In contrast, there were very many in liberal circles on the right wing, particularly among its activists, the Revisionists, who believed that the major part of the task and of the burden of building the country would devolve upon private initiative. Eventually, in the course of nature, some sort of compromise came about, arising from automatic forces such as the waves of mass aliyah, like the Fourth and Fifth Aliyahs, which brought private capital to the country and built the urban economy, and the immigration that laid the numerical basis for the building of the Yishuv.

But without the directing force of public capital; of national initiative; of the organized forces that were at the disposal of this initiative, such as the organized Workers' Movement in all its aspects: communal settlement, the Histadrut institutions, the youth movements, economic institutions, such as Solel Boneh, industry etc.; it is doubtful whether the Yishuv would have been able to stand the test of the national confrontation, for, in the 1930's, unlike the 1920's, the development was not carried on "by still waters." If ther were sings in the 1920's of "normal" development, that is the settlement of Europeans in an Asiatic country, as happened in other countries, these signs disappeared in the 1930's. The situation had changed in the 'thirties and by the beginning of the decade Zionism already confronted the Arab national movement. The first signs of an organized Arab national movement appeared in the disturbances of 1929. Toward the middle of the 1930's this movement grew in strength.

National forces and a national organization were needed to contend with the emergency situation that was created, and this was the principal contribution of the Zionist movement. All the experience that had been gained since the days of the Second Aliyah, since the year in which Ruppin founded the "Palestine Office," from the beginning of the workers' organization, from the first settlement collectives, from Degania, from the Histadrut, from the settlement of the Jezreel Valley, HaShomer, the Haganah, all that accumulated experience of organization and of collective action on behalf of the national interest, was put to the test in the years from 1931 to 1947. All this experience was available to the People of Israel and the national movement, and it is doubtful whether, without it, they would have achieved as much as they did.

Here we are faced with one of the paradoxes. Since the organized forces which were at the disposal of public initiative were mainly those of the Workers' Movement, there began to be convergence between the social aims of the Workers' Movement and the national aims. The two continued side by side. The movement which had hoped to build a different society in Eretz Israel, or, rather, to turn the Yishuv in Eretz Israel into a different society, a society based on equality and cooperation, did not succeed in this social mission. It established foundations and a nucleus for this different society in the cooperative settlement movement, the kibbutzim, the moshavim, and the Histadrut economy, but it did not turn the society of the Yishuv into a qualitatively different society. From this point of view, Yishuv society continued along the traditional Jewish lines, with changes in accordance with conditions.

But in the national sphere the success of this movement was almost complete. The movement, which from the days of the Second Aliyah had put itself at the service of the national interest, in defense, in settlement, in outreach, utterly exhausted its strength and its ability in the 'thirties and 'forties. It was what led the Yishuv toward the State, not only in the practical sense — that is a story in itself — but in the sense that it provided the instruments, the organizations, the groups of activists in different fields, defense, settlement, construction, who were ready to dedicate themselves to the national interest. It should be understood that the movement did not acquire this role leading to the State purely by accident, for it had intended to do so from the beginning. But it had intended to do so in two fields, the social and national, and nationally it achieved far more than it did socially.

105

XIII.

From a Minority Project to a Majority Enterprise — The Years Following the Establishment of the State

We shall end our study of Zionist construction precisely at the stage when Jewish settlement in Eretz Israel reached its peak. The struggle to establish the State lasted about ten years, from 1937 to 1947-8. All sections of the people and all its institutions took part in that struggle, the Workers' Movement, the underground, Etzel and Lehi, the new immigrants, and the Jewish people in the Diaspora who raised funds to finance the settlement and the struggle. After the foundation of the State a new period began, in which the test for the people was no longer to found the state but to build it.

With the foundation of the State, there occurred a substantial change in the relation between construction and policy. Until the State was established, construction was the means of realizing policy. Thenceforth, the State, through its institutions, became the framework and the means through which Zionist construction achieved one of its goals, to which it had aspired from the beginning — the achievement of sovereignty over construction in Eretz Israel.

With the achievement of sovereignty, a substantial change took place in the ability of Zionism to build its national home, for with the foundation of the State, Zionism achieved not only its longed-for political sovereignty, but sovereignty over the construction enterprise it had hoped for. During the Mandate years, at the time of the British rule in Eretz Israel, a bitter argument was conducted between the Zionists and the government over the scope of

106

immigration, the possibilities for land purchase, the import of capital, etc. From now on the Jewish national institutions had in their hands the control of immigration and of the land. From now on they would have complete authority to do whatever was within their power in Eretz Israel. In addition, in contrast to earlier periods, as a result of the war, because of the tragedy that befell the Jewish People and the foundation of the State, the national institutions were in possession of financial means of unprecedented size. From this time onwards, the relative balance between national and private capital was changed. If most of the development and growth in the towns had taken place, up to the foundation of the State, through the import of private capital, thenceforth most of the means for investment came from national capital, donated to the State of Israel by the Jews of the Diaspora, or from capital transferred to it as reparations by the German government, or as grants, or loans in aid, by the government of the United States.

The enterprise reached its peak, achieving unprecedented numbers, not only in comparison with Jewish settlement in Eretz Israel, but also in comparison with other settlement projects, both at that time and particularly in earlier periods.

The mass immigration of the years 1948 and 1953 was the realization of the Zionist dream of the gathering in of the exiles, of the absorption of multitudes of distressed Jews. For the first time in the history of Zionism, it was possible for it to achieve its goal, to provide an answer to Jewish distress. And indeed in 1948, the year of the war, 100,000 immigrants arrived in the country. The immigration reached its peak immediately after the War of Independence. In 1949 250,000 immigrants came to the country, and up to 1951 another 700,000 arrived. Within four years, more immigrants arrived in the country than the total Jewish population before the establishment of the State. The Yishuv doubled in size, from 700,000 to nearly a million and a half.

Apart from the numerical statistics, there was the harsh, and yet dramatic, reality of the meeting of immigrants from different lands, of the meeting of cultures and the conflicts between them, of the necessity of living together despite differences, of life in tents, which later became canvas and tin shacks, and the transition to housing developments, that spread across the face of the country. This was an immigration of those in need, from the refugee camps of Germany, from the ghettos of north Africa, from Iraq and from the Yemen. This aliyah, in all its variety and its vast dimensions, was absorbed mainly in the towns.

The urban settlement can be divided into three types. First of all, there was settlement in towns that had already had a large Jewish population before the establishment of the State. We refer here to the Hebrew cities like Tel Aviv, or the large Jewish communities in Jerusalem, Haifa, or Safed. These cities grew very rapidly. The second type included settlement in towns emptied of their Arab population, like Lydda, Ramle, or Acre. The third type was the development towns, established as part of the settlement program and as its continuation.

Some development towns were founded as urban settlements, the function of which was to provide services to their agricultural hinterland, like Kiryat Gat in the south and Kiryat Shmonah in the north. There were also towns that were intended as a spearhead for settlement at the southern tip of the country. From this time onwards, since the foundation of the State, development towns were added to settlement in kibbutzim and moshavim, as playing a national role in settling the borders and in filling in the geographical gaps in the country. *The development towns became the national settlement arm of national policy after the establishment of the State.*

As is natural, in recent years the main effort has been put into providing housing and employment for the immigrants. This led to an enormous building program, enormous by international standards, financed mainly from the national budget. And this led to the great and comprehensive effort to develop industry, both in order to provide jobs and employ large numbers of immigrants who could not live only on agriculture, and in order to improve the economy of the country, so that it should not be dependent on grants and contributions from Diaspora Jewry for ever. At first the State's balance of payments was very negative, but we have gone a long way in industrial development, and this is one of the greatest revolutions of Zionism, which should also be included in the saga of settlement.

The wave of mass immigration, which declined noticeably in 1953, was renewed in 1955 and reached another peak in 1957, when 70,000 immigrants arrived in the country. That was, in effect, the end of mass immigration. The first stage of the absorption of mass immigration ended in the mid-fifties, and with it the hardest social and economic trial that the Yishuv, the Zionist movement and the State of Israel had to face throughout their history.

In addition to urban settlement, settlement on the land and the development of agriculture were the second great test of the construction enterprise. This settlement was, without doubt, the crowning achievement of the national effort, not for its numbers, nor for its contribution to the absorption of the immigrants, but because the personal trials of the new immigrants, who arrived in their thousands at that time and went into agriculture, were so much more severe than those of the immigrants who were absorbed in the various kinds of urban settlements.

The pace of agricultural settlement was astonishing and unprecedented. It was remarkable even in comparison with the 1930's, the "Tower and Stockade" period. Within four years, more than 300 settlements, kibbutzim, moshavim and moshavot, were established. Within four years the same number of settlements were founded as had been created by Jewish settlement in Eretz Israel from the First Aliyah to the establishment of the State.

Most of the new immigrant settlements, more than 200 out of the 300, were moshavim. They are evidence of the decisive part played by the new aliyah in the settlement of Eretz Israel. This was the enterprise of immigrants who came mainly from Asia and Africa, and was their great and important contribution to Zionist construction. In the Galilee or the Lachish area, west or east, the new immigrants made their decisive contribution everywhere.

The importance and the dimensions of the settlement enterprise in Eretz Israel, which we have described in these chapters, was unparalleled in the history of the Jewish people, but, in order to assess it properly, it should be compared not only with similar projects in the history of our people, principally those carried on at the same time as that of Zionism, such as the settlement in Argentina, or the attempts to settle Jews in Soviet Russia, in the Crimea, or later, further east, in Birobidjan — all projects which failed. The settlement in Eretz Israel should be compared with settlement enterprises attempted by other states and other nations in the world.

Zionist settlement can be divided into two periods, the period preceding the establishment of the State, and the period that followed it. It is true that the settlement before the setting up of the State laid the foundations of the Jewish Yishuv in Eretz Israel and of the Jewish State, but it was rather limited in comparison with the comprehensive settlement that followed the establishment of the State. If we compare this limited project with similar attempts by other nations, we can better assess its value. For example, in the nineteenth century, Germany attempted to settle German citizens in its colonies in Africa. Despite its efforts, it succeeded in settling only 20,000 Germans during twenty years of settlement. Japan planned to settle 100,000 Japanese peasant families in Manchuria within ten years, as the start of a very big settlement program. In the end, by the eve of the Second World War, 100,000 individual Japanese had settled in Manchuria, not 100,000 families, and certainly not millions the Japanese had intended to settle in that time. The Italian settlement attempt in north Africa lasted fifty years and at its end 250,000 Italians had settled there. Australia also tried to set up a big settlement program, which did not succeed despite the fact that it lasted about ten years. These failures stand out against a background of large territories, cheap land, natural resources, as well as the government support which these projects enjoyed. In comparison, Zionism succeeded in building up, in the years of its operation before the foundation of the state, a population of about 600,000 people, among them more than 400,000 immigrants who came to the country at that time, and all this under incomparably more difficult conditions than those of the other projects. Only one settlement project at that time exceeded

Zionist settlement in numbers, the exchange of populations between Greece and Turkey after the First World War. Within a very short space of time — a year and a half — about 1,300,000 Greeks migrated or were expelled from Turkey to Greece, and about 400,000 Turks from Greece to Turkey.

If we compare the settlement enterprise after the foundation of the State, which was unparalleled in its dimensions and its scope and in the problems involved in it, with the settlement preceding the establishment of the State, together they make up one of the greatest settlement enterprises in human history.

It is important to distinguish between a settlement enterprise and countries that absorb immigration. Immigration-absorbing countries took in more immigrants, both relatively and absolutely. But here we are speaking of a settlement enterprise by migrants, and this is a very important point. Perhaps more than in any other country of immigration or settlement enterprise, the building here depended mainly on the immigrants who came, because the country is poor in natural resources and its land is limited. The building was done mainly by these people who came, in one way or another, and built up the Yishuv.

I have referred to these lectures as "From Rosh Pina to Dimona." North of Rosh Pina lie Kiryat Shmonah and Metula. South of Dimona lie Yehoram and Eilat. This is the story of Jewish settlement. This is a story with a historic dimension, which has continued for eighty years, and perhaps even longer. It is a story with a cultural dimension, since the various waves of immigrants, from the First Aliyah to the mass aliyah after the establishment of the State, though belonging, it is true, to the same people and the same religion, were very different from each other in culture. Not only were their languages different, but their yearnings and their spiritual equipment were different too. It is a story of generations, since people of different ages took part in this enterprise, people with families and the young. It is a story of ideas and of ideologies, since people with different world views came here. There were those who came because of romantic motives; there were those who came for self-redemption; there were others who tried to build Utopias,

111

perfect societies, or a perfect Jewish society in Eretz Israel; there were those who simply came to work in Eretz Israel, to live there and to fulfill the commandment to work the land; there were dreamers and there were realists. All these aspects of culture, origin, age, ideas and periods led to a great problematic variety. This variety was problematic in the past and is still problematic in the present. It has caused conflict and tensions, but its great test was in the fact of its ability to continue to operate, in the fact of its ability to carry on the settlement enterprise. The duration of the enterprise from 1882 to 1957, or until the end of the 1950's, about eighty years of settlement, was its main test. This was the test of the voluntary movement and of its institutions which planned, directed and carried out as elaborate and wide-ranging a settlement enterprise as it became by its end. This is evidence both for the strength of the people who took part in it, and for the power of the movement that directed it.

In the history of the Yishuv in Eretz Israel and the history of the State, there were wars which left scars, and there were struggles which were like the froth on the surface of flowing water, which soon passed and were forgotten. The main thing which has endured and has determined the image of this society, in the past, in the present and also in the future, has been the constructive enterprise, the building enterprise. The way in which the society and the state were built for good or for ill, determines our present and will also determine our future.